Aspects of modern sociology

The social structure of modern Britain

GENERAL EDITORS

John Barron Mays
Eleanor Rathbone Professor of Social Science, University of Liverpool

Maurice Craft
Senior Lecturer in Education, University of Exeter

The Working Class

Gordon Rose B.Sc. (Econ.), B.Litt., Ph.D.

Reader in Social Administration
University of Manchester

Longmans

LONGMANS, GREEN AND CO. LTD
London and Harlow

Associated companies, branches and representatives throughout the world

© *Longmans, Green and Co. Ltd 1968*
First published 1968

Printed in Great Britain by
Spottiswoode, Ballantyne and Co. Ltd.
London and Colchester

Contents

Editors' Preface

British higher education is now witnessing a very rapid expansion of teaching and research in the social sciences, and, in particular, in sociology. This new series has been designed for courses offered by universities, colleges of education, colleges of technology, and colleges of further education to meet the needs of students training for social work, teaching and a wide variety of other professions. It does not attempt a comprehensive treatment of the whole field of sociology, but concentrates on the social structure of modern Britain which forms a central feature of most university and college sociology courses in this country. Its purpose is to offer an analysis of our contemporary society through the study of basic demographic, ideological and structural features, and through the study of such major social institutions as the family, education, the economic and political structure, and so on.

The aim has been to produce a series of introductory texts which will in combination form the basis for a sustained course of study, but each volume has been designed as a single whole and can be read in its own right.

We hope that the topics covered in the series will prove attractive to a wide reading public and that, in addition to students, others who wish to know more than is readily available about the nature and structure of their own society will find them of interest.

JOHN BARRON MAYS
MAURICE CRAFT

Introduction

Although the term 'the working class' appears in the title of this book, and is used elsewhere in the text, it should not be taken too seriously as a sociological description. The term 'class' has a precise meaning in sociology, and for the most part it has not been employed in this strict sense; and since most people work no matter what class they belong to, the description 'working' is no real help. Nevertheless the term 'working class' has become generally associated with manual workers, and only the professional sociologist is likely to cavil.

Most of the information used here comes from a limited number of studies of the British working class, and in order to save repetition, they have been referred to either by author or by the place in which the study was carried out. There are also a number of other studies often quoted and these are designated by the author's name. Much of the data is competently summarised and annotated in the following book referred to throughout as 'Klein':

J. Klein, *Samples from English Cultures*, 2 vols, Routledge, 1965.

The major studies on social stratification and mobility used are:

D. V. Glass, ed., *Social Mobility in Britain*, Routledge, 1954.

K. Svalastoga, *Prestige, Class and Mobility*, Heinemann, 1959.

(This latter is a Danish study, but is available in English, and is highly competent and sophisticated.)

Labour Mobility Survey—Government Social Survey: *Labour Mobility in Great Britain 1953–63*, by A. I. Harris and R. Clausen, H.M.S.O. 1966.

The rest of the studies often quoted are shown below, with a brief note on each.

ASHTON—N. Dennis, F. Henriques and C. Slaughter, *Coal is Our Life*, Eyre & Spottiswoode, 1956.

Ashton is a fictitious name for a small town (14,000) in the West Riding of Yorkshire, with two-thirds of its male workers coal miners. No sampling.

BANBURY—Margaret Stacey, *Tradition and Change*, O.U.P. 1960.

Town of 19,000 in Oxfordshire. General study mainly concerned with contrasting those native to the town and those who have moved to it. Sample of 1,015 households with basic information, 50 families studied intensively, and some streets.

BETHNAL GREEN—M. Young and P. Willmott, *Family and Kinship in East London*, Routledge, 1957; Penguin.

Sample of 993 adults for basic information; 45 families with two or more children under 15 studied intensively. On Greenleigh, an overspill estate, 47 families of the same constitution, and 41 of them re-interviewed two years later.

BRANCH STREET—M. Paneth, *Branch Street*, Allen & Unwin, 1944.

Very acute observation of families at the very bottom of the working class in an area of Paddington, London.

COVENTRY—L. Kuper, ed., *Living in Towns*, Cresset Press, 1953.

Town planning study, with a detailed analysis of 90 families in a street on a new estate, Braydon Road. Also an overspill study, two on leisure, and one on play of children in flats.

CROWN STREET—C. Vereker, J. B. Mays, E. Gittus and M. Broady, *Urban Redevelopment and Social Change*, Liverpool University Press, 1961.

Sample survey of 574 heads of households in a slum area of Liverpool, covering housing, family and kinship, leisure, shopping, education.

DAGENHAM—P. Willmott, *The Evolution of a Community*, Routledge, 1963.

Continuation of the Institute of Community Studies' work in Bethnal Green. Sample survey of 877 adults over 21. Comparable family sample of 50. Sample of 20 tenants who had arrived on the estate in 1930 or before. Accent on family and kinship, but also on rehousing policy.

LIVERPOOL—G. D. Mitchell and T. Lupton, 'The Liverpool Estate', in *Neighbourhood and Community* (symposium) Liverpool University Press, 1954.

Sample survey of 98 men and 148 women, of which 75 men and their wives mainly used, on a housing estate in Liverpool created for wartime factory workers. More detailed study of three blocks of twelve houses each; and of the Residents' Association.

NOTTINGHAM—J. Newson and E. Newson, *Patterns of Infant Care in an Urban Community*, Allen & Unwin, 1963; Penguin.

Sample survey of 709 mothers of one-year-old children in Nottingham, interviewed within a fortnight, either way, of the first birthday. Also *Four Years Old in an Urban Community*, Allen & Unwin, 1968, published too late to be included in this text.

OXFORD—J. M. Mogey, *Family and Neighbourhood*, O.U.P. 1956.

Comparison of a working class area of Oxford and a housing estate on the outskirts. Thirty households interviewed from each, plus additional information on other small samples, and an analysis of the Housing Department Records of the 1,006 families on the Barton Estate. Intended as a pilot survey, but never followed up (not the author's fault).

RADBY—W. J. H. Sprott, Pearl Jephcott and M. P. Carter, *The Social Background of Delinquency*, University of Nottingham, 1954. Unpublished, but copies available in some libraries and there should be a microfilm at least in all of the larger libraries.

Comparative study of high and low delinquency streets in a small mining town in Nottinghamshire (fictitious name; population, 23,000). Interviews in 225 households, covering the streets concerned, partly by taking every tenth house, partly by introductions; working and taking part in activities in the town; a playroom in one of the worst streets. Acute observation, but limited quantitative data.

SHEFFIELD—M. W. Hodges and C. S. Smith, 'The Sheffield Estate', the other study in *Neighbourhood and Community* (see 'Liverpool' above).

A Council estate in Sheffield first started in 1926. Sample survey of 156 housewives, by address and the house on each side of it, and thus some useful material on neighbours; general study of the estate.

3

SHIP STREET—M. Kerr, *The People of Ship Street*, Routledge, 1958.

Another study of a small area of the Liverpool slums, cast in social psychological terms. Contacts with about 60 families, apparently almost exclusively with the women; no sampling.

SWANSEA—C. Rosser and C. Harris, *The Family and Social Change*, Routledge, 1965.

A parallel study to Bethnal Green in Swansea. Sample survey of 1,962 adults over 21; mainly on family and kinship but more comprehensive than Bethnal Green.

WOODFORD—P. Willmott and M. Young, *Family and Class in a London Suburb*, Routledge, 1960.

Comparison of Bethnal Green and Woodford, a mainly middle-class London suburb, on the same lines as the other work of the Institute of Community Studies. Three samples; 210 people of pensionable age, drawn from the records in six doctors' practices; 939 drawn randomly from the electoral register (adults over 21), 50 families comparable with the previous studies.

GORER—G. Gorer, *Exploring English Character*, Cresset Press, 1955.

Result of a questionnaire filled in voluntarily by readers of *The People*, a popular Sunday newspaper, in 1951: 10,500 were returned; and 5,000 coded. These comprise all the married men (760) and married women (533) without children, and a randomly selected group to reproduce the marital status distribution in the English population over sixteen. Heavily skewed towards younger people and males and towards the more literate in each section of the population. Also a quota sample of 1,760. Questions cover a wide range, but mainly beliefs and attitudes.

HOGGART—R. Hoggart, *The Uses of Literacy*, Chatto & Windus, 1957; Penguin.

Evocative, sensitive, and well written analysis of working class life from the author's own experience.

SEABROOK—J. Seabrook, *The Unprivileged*, Longmans, 1967.

Similar to Hoggart, but concentrating more on previous generations of the author's family.

ZWEIG—F. Zweig, *The Worker in an Affluent Society*, Heinemann, 1961.

Six hundred interviews with workers in five firms. Rather less impressionistic than his earlier work, but the choice of sample puts it preponderantly into the upper half of the working class.

This list does not, of course, exhaust the material, but it contains all the studies conducted with some degree of care and sophistication, particularly by the use of sampling. It should be noted, however, that most of the samples from which the more detailed information is drawn, are very small—the direct result of limited resources and the poor organisation of the facilities for work of this kind in England. The main outlines of the results are thus clear enough, but there has so far been little or none of the narrowing of the field for more detailed and systematic study which is the essence of scientific progress. If, therefore, speculation reigns in many parts of this book, it is because there is no other recourse.

The list above also contains the two accounts I have found most useful by people who can write (and few sociologists can); and who therefore can convey more clearly the realities of working-class life as it is experienced by those who live it. Several novels and plays are referred to in the text, but the demands of the story and character-isation tend to distort the picture presented of working-class life. Additional material with a more specialised bearing on particular aspects, is given in the Reference and Reading Lists for each chapter (see pp. 136–45), which are so arranged as to include the main studies in each field.

Plan of the book

The book starts with a brief discussion of the appropriateness of the background of sociological theory to the analysis of the working class, and this is expanded in the last chapter. It would have been out of place in this type of book to discuss this at length, but it would be equally out of place not to remind the reader of the underlying problems of analysis. There is then a critical summary of the information about occupation and stratification. The third chapter expands in more detail the worker's experience at work. The next continues the examination of the major determinants by discussing income, education, health and housing. A short sketch of traditional working-class life as it emerges from the descriptive studies introduces two chapters on the family and the life cycle, followed by a more detailed look at the young and the old. The next four chapters cover leisure, religion, politics and deviance.

It has been found necessary to treat each 'subject' to some extent independently, and to deal with history, present situation, and the changes which appear to be taking place, together; because of the brevity of the sections, this inevitably leads to some jerkiness. An attempt is made to bring the strands together in the final chapter, in which changes and future trends are summarised and considered in relation to the analytical orientation with which the book began.

The unfortunate but conscientious author who essays even a small book on the working class finds himself in the immediate difficulty that the theoretical structure upon which most work in the field of social stratification and social class is based is ill adapted to his purpose. It has been the practice of sociologists to stand back, and with a grand sweep of the unblinking, objective eye, consider the whole of society as a series of related strata. Some sociologists have been primarily interested to see why strata exist, and what functions they serve, usually in the assumption that all the components of the social fabric have some purpose and fit together.[1] Others have been more interested in power and the way it is handled and preserved.[2] The best known and by far the most influential theory is, of course, the Marx–Engels approach which concentrates primarily on class opposition, particularly in economic terms.

If, however, one considers only these people who fit roughly into the various categories of manual workers—which is what is usually meant by 'the working class', these approaches are less helpful. Since we are only looking at part of a society, we can hardly expect to see the same kind of functional whole (even if it is believed that a functional analysis is sufficient), and while one can say in a general sense that skilled, semiskilled and unskilled workers do depend on each other, it is no sense a one-sided dependence of the kind discussed by Ossowski.[3]

It is also not of any great assistance to think in terms of power or élites within the working class, although the power of others over them is a very important factor. There is a sense in which the top section of the working class are, and regard themselves, as an élite, but they can hardly be said as a stratum to exercise power over the lower strata. Indeed, if one thinks in terms of trade union strengths, it is rather the other way round. There are, of course, foremen and supervisors, but they tend to be people of extremely limited power, operating within strata, rather than as a separate stratum. Furthermore, while some conflict undoubtedly exists between strata, it is diffuse, and bears no relation to the Marxist analysis of class conflict.

We could, of course, avoid all the important questions by simply accepting the fact that there are a number of ways in which we can define the existence of hierarchies of prestige, particularly in occupation and income, and confine ourselves to a description of consistencies and differences. Much of this book is, in fact, of this nature. We cannot, however, examine the nature of social change without some sort of framework in which to set the changes concerned. It is impossible in a limited space to set up anything like a comprehensive framework, and only a few points of some importance are made.

Perhaps one should start by looking again at the whole range of strata not from the outside nor from the top, but from the bottom. The first question which then springs to mind is why anybody ever accepts an underprivileged position. No one surely can escape the fact that they are nearer the bottom than the top of the pile, and the studies we shall be looking at concerning prestige hierarchies tend to confirm strongly that most people know there is a pile and are prepared to see themselves as having a place in it. It is surely a most important question for the understanding of the working class to establish how a person in that position legitimates low status and poverty, especially in societies which are consciously egalitarian such as our own, and where opportunities are present for advancement. As a result of 'The Rise of the Meritocracy' the problem of legitimation of low status becomes increasingly acute, as Michael Young[4] points out.

We can distinguish a number of possible reasons for acceptance of low status.

1. *Power.* Belief in the ultimate power of those of higher status to harm, whether by force or by magic; in this world, or in a magical or religious other world; by fair trial or arbitrarily.

2. *Helplessness.* A consequence of power—failure to identify any remotely practical way of changing the system—this is, of course, the basis of public order in *apartheid*—'There's nothing you can do about it, so why try?'

3. *Restricted referents.* Learning, usually from early childhood, to compare oneself only with a very limited range of people who are very much like oneself. In this way, the higher strata hardly come into one's reckoning.

4. *Selective rationalisation.* Selection of those aspects of one's status which are positive and of general high value throughout the whole society—'We are decent, honest, hardworking people.'

5. *Feelings of limited worth.* A steadfast belief in one's own very limited worth as against others—only possible to those who take joy in submission.

6. *Acculturation processes.* The ways in which the above are conveyed to child, adolescent and adult, and turned into an acceptable system.

It will be obvious that these are of somewhat different orders. Numbers 1 and 2 are mainly concerned with the political, economic and social structure; 3-6 are to do with the process of growing up and establishing oneself in the community, and indeed 3, 4 and 5 might be regarded as sub-orders of 6; 3 and 4 are part of the process of status maintenance; and 5 may be heavily socially induced (as in women, and in some of the older generation brought up in the habits of deference), or may be an individual personality trait.

Numbers 3 and 4 can be regarded as part of the continuing process of maintenance, but also as adaptive mechanisms. The normal situation is that the current social order is accepted by most people, even though it may be regarded as imperfect or unjust in a number of respects. Deficiencies in acculturation, changes in referents, and in the selection of rationalisations are the major forces for change and we shall return to these, although very briefly, at a later stage.

The concept of referents (conventionally called reference groups although they need not be groups) is of vital importance in the understanding of much working-class behaviour. Feelings of deprivation are not necessarily related to the degree of deprivation as measured by the disinterested observer; they are much more a question of the reactions of the deprived, and these are largely governed by standards of comparison. It is possible to see oneself as very much better off than before, better off than those below you on some selected status hierarchy ('So long as you've got your health . . .'), (*relative advantage*); or worse off than you were before, and worse off than the people above you (*relative deprivation*). A wider range of referents upwards gives room for higher aspirations, a *displacement of referents* into areas not related to the main sources of prestige, can act as an opiate ('You too can have muscles like mine!'). The manipulation of this system, in conjunction with the mechanism of selective rationalisation, plays an important part both in the support of the *status quo* and in effecting change.

Density of relationships

A second area of importance, recently discussed at length by Frankenberg,[5] is the amount people see of each other, the range of roles in which they meet each other, and the strength of ties with kin and non-kin. For convenience, these are described here under the generic term of *density of relationships*. Most of the studies made of the working class in recent years have been primarily concerned with problems in this area.

The typical high density situation is illustrated by an account of a short shopping trip, recorded in the Bethnal Green study, in which the informant met fourteen people she knew, most of them well enough to tell the research worker something about their lives. In a week, the same informant saw sixty-three people she knew, of whom thirty-eight were related to at least one other person in the total. High density of relationships depends mainly upon two things: low mobility covering several generations, and extended families: but it is pushed even higher by extension over a range of roles as happens in Ashton, where relationships deriving from work and non-work roles are interwoven because of the dominant position of a single workplace. It is, however, important to distinguish between general familiarity with a number of local people on an acquaintanceship basis; friendship; and kinship. A close-knit community does not necessarily have a large number of very close and all pervading ties and may consist mainly of general contacts, leading to a sense of familiarity—of belonging because 'you know so many people'. A distinction must be drawn, therefore, between *general contacts* and *close relationships*. Either of these may or may not exist against a background of *multiple role relationships*; where, as in the Ashton example, people see each other a great deal, not simply because of proximity but in a number of different activities in which they all take part.

Lockwood has recently described three types of worker, the proletarian, the deferential, and the privatised.[6] It is not very clear whether he means to divide the whole of the working class into these three groups, but it seems unlikely from his descriptions. Briefly, the proletarian and the deferential both belong to the traditional working class, the proletarian being associated with industrial communities, such as mining and shipbuilding, which are sufficiently distinctive and old-established to give him a strong consciousness of his membership of the working class and its traditions of struggle. His political affiliation is Labour or further left. He tends to live in an area of high density of relationships and interlocked work and non-work roles, and thus inhabits a kind of working-class island.

The deferential worker is less likely to be in this type of situation. He thinks largely in terms of prestige and leadership and accepts the leadership of his 'betters', the people who know how to run things, although sometimes he sees them as spurious leaders with misguided followers (often of the proletarian type). The term 'he' has been used, but in fact deferential workers are much more likely to be women, to be elderly and to have low incomes. Apparently they live in areas of high density relationships, but themselves have lower densities.

The privatised worker, first distinguished in an earlier study[7], is much more concerned with money and possessions. He has usually reduced his density of relationships by moving out of the traditional working-class areas, often into suburban housing estates. He still remains working-class in many aspects of thought and behaviour, but he has no real class consciousness and is concerned only with himself, his home and his family; achieving status in a wilderness of neat, well kept, well stocked houses, by seeing that his house is a little better than the next.

It is not by any means clear how far these stereotypes represent large sections of the working class, or how far they are small patches amongst the mass of less distinctive working-class lives.

It must not be forgotten that there are other factors which may well be of considerable importance. The rapid changes since World War II have created a gap between the younger and the older generations; this tends to crop up in a number of contexts and may well be of considerable importance. Similarly, locality is often very important—whether the family lives in the older areas of the big towns, or has been redeveloped into the new sprawling suburbs, or if they live in a small town in the transitional working-class areas (mainly in the north), or in the hedged prosperity of the commuting zone which spreads over a good deal of the south. These points also contribute to the difficulty of describing what we mean by *the* working class.

Stratification by occupational prestige

Stratification derives directly from the social consequences of individual differences. Ranking is seen to some extent in animals—herd leadership, pecking orders in chickens—but this lacks the essential element of recognition of some sense of identity with others on the same level. In man, social interaction reinforces the awareness of likeness between equals, and of dissimilarities between strata. This awareness need not necessarily be marked, but it undoubtedly exists. The sociologist's very imperfect ability to measure identification accurately makes social strata as he states them something of an artefact, but he also has plenty of evidence that people do see these strata to a considerable degree as social realities.

Pretty well every human characteristic or relationship has some degree of variability, and criteria can be set up against which it can be ranked. Many rankings have no context of social evaluation, for example some people have longer forefingers than others, and one can rank people according to the length of their forefingers, but there is no suggestion that those with longer forefingers are in any sense better or worse, above or below others in social standing. In terms of social behaviour, however, a wide range of activities are seen by most people as bearing different amounts of prestige. This leads to a ranking of specific sections of behaviour in terms of social status. It is impossible to avoid connotations of top and bottom, better and worse, in the hierarchical aspects of social status. Although the term can be used in other ways, we shall use 'status' here as a shorthand for social status and it denotes a position in a socially evaluated hierarchy.

Since many actions can be ranked, from having a pottery rustic figure in the window of one's front room (an indication of respectability in the traditional working class), to income and type of work; there are a variety of possible continua and a single person, or family, may hold different positions relative to the top and bottom on each of a number of criteria. We can connect up a number of these into a status profile, and a collection of people with similar profiles form a stratum.

In practice we do not do this. We find some socially important characteristic which is bound to have a great deal of influence on the way of life of the person possessing it and his dependants, and we then assume that many of the other things follow. We find in a very general way, that the main determinants are closely related (occupation, income, level of education, people's views of their own and other people's general standing in the community),[8] and we thus tend to pick a single, easily obtainable characteristic as an indicator of all others and of the relationship in which they stand—usually occupation. It should be remembered that these relationships hold only over large samples, or in very broad comparisons in smaller samples, and their predictive power of the place the person holds on other status hierarchies is often uncertain and sometimes totally unknown. In the working class, occupational prestige is probably a less good predictor than in the middle class.

There can obviously be some dispute about the comparative prestige of occupations, [9] but, in extended comparisons, both Inkeles and

Rossi,[10] and Svalastoga found high correlations between rank orders in different countries. Svalastoga finds a correlation of 0·9 (which is extremely high) between United States, British, Dutch and Danish rankings; although the social distance between manual and non-manual occupations was smaller in the United States than in Europe.

One must accept as a fact, therefore, that when given lists of occupations covering all classes, most people in industrialised countries put them in the same prestige order. It is less clear whether this applies to manual workers ranking manual jobs. In the first place, the studies show some tendency for specific strata to magnify their own type of job in relation to those nearby. Secondly, they show more variation in ranking by manual workers, especially among the unskilled. Young and Willmott,[11] in a small study, found that manual workers tended to put skilled manual above junior non-manual occupations and they also found a substantial minority who put manual work at the top of the list because of its social utility—an example of variation in referents. Nevertheless, we are probably justified in talking in general terms of a hierarchy of strata represented by occupation, so long as we remember that statement of a particular type of occupation is no more than a somewhat uncertain indicator of other types of behaviour, especially when talking about the working class.

Classification of occupation

The classifications most generally used are those of the Census. They suffer from numerous problems of definition and interpretation into which we cannot go here.[12] The five groups which have been most used, and are referred to in the Census as 'social class' groupings are well known, but the 1951 and 1961 Census introduced a further classification into 'socio-economic groups', seventeen of these in the 1961 Census. There are differences in definition and grouping from one Census to another and comparisons are hazardous.

The working class is usually taken to refer to manual workers, that is, skilled, semiskilled, unskilled ('Social Classes' III, IV, and V; but this particular grading, which is based on occupational rather than individual categorisation, mixes manual and non-manual together in the middle grades). The socio-economic groups (SEG) are more widely used in the 1961 Census, and are more accurate, and, in these, 8–11 inclusive and 15 (agricultural workers) cover manual workers. There remain a number of uncertainties in the form of personal service workers, own account workers, the armed forces and possibly some of the junior manual workers.

Nevertheless the manual/non-manual division has been much justified and widely used,[13] and most of the major analyses have been made in these terms. In discussing them, however, it is important to remember that there can be a difference of 10 per cent or more of the population categorised if the other categories are added in; and that many of the 17 per cent economically active and the 13 per cent inactive males unassigned in the 1961 tables really belong to the working class, assuming that these are for the most part randomly distributed enumerators' errors. Taking the narrow definition, 60 per cent of the male population in work, and 50 per cent of those not in work (mainly retired) would count as manual workers, agricultural workers contributing only about 2·5 per cent in each category in England and Wales. Of the economically active, this figure is made up of 3·3 per cent foremen and supervisors, 31·6 per cent skilled, 14·7 per cent semiskilled, 8·3 per cent unskilled and 2·3 per cent agricultural workers.

Lockwood has considered at some length the history and recent experience of the black-coated worker,[14] and has emphasised the gradual decline of earnings differentials, and the increasing routinis-ation of clerical work so that it becomes large-scale, unskilled and repetitive, and without any of the close contact with superiors and possibilities for advancement which characterised the nineteenth-century clerical worker. He also emphasises the difference in allegi-ance and outlook between office and factory floor workers. The posi-tion is made extremely complex by the fact that many children of skilled manual workers are in low-grade non-manual positions, and the increasing number of women clerical workers and secretaries further obscures the manual/non-manual distinction.

The Labour Mobility Survey very wisely divides the Registrar

General's 'social classes' III (Skilled) and IV (Partly-skilled) into non-manual and manual groups and treats these separately. The non-manual Class IV is not very important so far as men is concerned, comprising 2·6 per cent of all men in 1963 but there were 12·2 per cent of the women in this category and 5·9 per cent of all workers covered. Probably the best we can do is to draw a line between non-manual and manual Class III, and consider all those below the line as working class. This gives us 72 per cent of the men in 1953, and 70 per cent in 1963; of the women 54 per cent and 51 per cent, and both sexes 66 per cent and 64 per cent.

We have surprisingly little information about the 'own account' group, but this must surely contain a considerable number of corner shop owners who are very similar in every way to the people they serve (except that they work longer hours and often earn less, which is the price of 'independence'). Similarly many of the personal service workers must also be working class people. It is, however, impossible to distinguish between those who are and who are not, or to guess at the proportion, and they have not been included, at least as far as the figures go.

Routh,[15] in a study covering the Censuses of 1911–51, has recast the Census information into 'occupational classes' (*not* the same as any of the Census groupings), and shows that the proportion of foremen and supervisors has increased steadily from 1·3 per cent in 1911 to 2·6 per cent in 1951, while skilled manual workers have shown a steady fall. The proportion of semiskilled workers rose between 1921 and 1931 but has fallen off overall, and that of unskilled workers has fallen since 1931. A comparison with the United States shows slightly higher proportions of foremen and skilled workers in Great Britain over the whole period and about the same proportion of semiskilled and unskilled workers.

Some of these changes are due to differences in the distribution between industrial groups as particular types of industry progress or decline. These have led to a substantial reduction in the semiskilled, and a slight increase in the proportion of the unskilled, while they have not affected the skilled.

Going back to the 1961 Census, SEGs 8–11 plus 15, we find that these represented 52 per cent of all households, 57 per cent of all people in households, 59 per cent of all earners, and 58 per cent of all children in households. In each of these cases by far the largest group are the skilled workers, and the second largest unskilled workers.

Social mobility

Since the data upon upward and downward social mobility is mainly in terms of occupation, it is appropriate to deal with it here. The information is cast in terms of occupational strata and movement between them: there is less information about movements within strata. Data is also available upon changes in educational achievement and income, but these also are usually given in relation to occupational strata.

In general, studies in various countries have found a high degree of mobility between father and son upwards and downwards across the manual/non-manual line. The Lipset and Bendix study shows that in the industrialised countries for which we have soundly based information (U.S.A., Germany, Sweden, Japan, France, Switzerland, Denmark, Great Britain and Italy), from one generation to another a quarter to a third of the non-farm population moves across this line, and they are remarkably similar in the rates shown, although they vary in the degree of upward mobility (apparently highest in Switzerland, and low in Great Britain), and downward mobility (apparently very high in Great Britain and very low in Switzerland). It is interesting to note that the United States falls somewhere in the middle on the measures of upward mobility. Despite these variations, there appears in general to be more similarity than difference in the occupational structures and relatively high mobility patterns in these countries and this seems to be related to their degree of industrialisation.

It is much more difficult to obtain information about mobility within the manual grades, since a great deal depends on skill classification. The partly skilled or semiskilled group is particularly subject to variation in definition, and international comparisons are unreliable. Much of what is said below is thus drawn from Glass's large-scale British study supplemented by the more recent Social Survey Labour Mobility Study. The Glass study is based on a sample taken in 1949 of men aged eighteen and over and it may well be that mobility rates have changed in subsequent cohorts. They do not, however, seem to have changed to any substantial degree in the birth cohorts covered by the Glass study.

Before looking at this it is necessary to remember that the actual numbers in each stratum at different periods are no guide to the members who may have moved up or down. The number of seats in the theatre does not change but the people sitting in them may well do so. Furthermore, the opportunity to move depends on the number of jobs available; it is much more difficult to be an unskilled worker if the number of unskilled jobs is radically cut. The result may be unemployment, or it may be a considerable increase in the semi-skilled. There is, however, a more subtle point; the possibility of moving depends also upon the relative size of the stratum concerned in relation to others at the point at which the cross-sectional cut (the sample) is taken.

The point is important because the Glass study shows apparently contradictory results in relation to the largest stratum (skilled manual and routine grades of non-manual workers). A direct comparison between father's and son's occupations shows this stratum as having the highest degree of stability with about half the sons falling into the same stratum throughout the range of birth cohorts of fathers and sons. This is dependent on the total make-up of the hierarchy of strata, and it distorts the picture of rates of mobility in each strata. If a statistical technique is applied to nullify the effect of variations in size, it turns out that the stratum mentioned has the highest rate of mobility: the turnover as compared with other occupational strata is consistently greater.

Which of these conclusions one uses depends upon the purpose one wishes to serve. The important point in the present context is the degree to which there is a consciousness in one generation of having done better or worse than the last, irrespective of why this has happened, and this leads one to an analysis in terms of direct relationship between father and son—the first conclusion. In the working class the lifetime occupational stratum tends to be set fairly early so that the relative ages of father and son are less important, although there is some evidence that with increasing age, a number of those in the semiskilled and unskilled categories who had previously been ranked higher, fall back again (combination of the two bottom categories makes it difficult to suggest reasons).

The results show that of the fathers who were unskilled, only 27 per cent had unskilled sons, while 23 per cent were semiskilled and 36 per cent skilled; 31 per cent of the sons of the semiskilled were in the same category, 15 per cent were unskilled and 39 per cent skilled. In the skilled category, 47 per cent were the same, 17 per cent had become semiskilled and 12 per cent unskilled, while 12 per cent had gone up into the lowest non-manual grade. The proportion in the higher non-manual grades is probably less reliable as it is affected by differences in ages amongst the sons as it usually takes time to rise a long way. The major proportions who have moved tend not to move far, but a third of the unskilled have become skilled (or routine non-manual?), far more of the semiskilled had gone up than down, and the movers amongst the skilled had gone up and down in roughly equal proportions. For comparison, just under 40 per cent of those in the highest non-manual class had sons in that class, and just over 20 per cent were in manual grades.

We do not have any similar information relating to a more recent sample, but the Labour Mobility Study provides a comparison of occupational status of the same workers in 1953 and 1963. This confirms the tendency for the unskilled to rise (nearly one in three men did so) and one in five of the male workers in the semiskilled category also rose. The skilled manual category again presents a much more stable aspect. In the higher non-manual groups there has been much less movement. While unskilled women have risen in about the same proportion as the men, they have a much stronger tendency to fall in the lower categories, and particularly move downwards from the skilled manual stratum. Unfortunately, there is no age breakdown so that one cannot tell if there is any change over age cohorts.

Other classifications

Both in Coventry and in Banbury it was found that the people questioned tended to divide the working class into three, a very respectable group at the top, a 'rough' group at the bottom, and the rest. These did not entirely correspond with the occupational skill divisions, but they did so in a rough way. The samples about which detailed information were collected were quite small, and do not show much differentiation between the various strata within the working class.

In Radby five gradings were constructed on the basis of house-keeping standards, husband/wife relationship, relationship with children, and education. The earners here were overwhelmingly miners and there is no very clear relationship with occupation. There is no indication, however, what their occupational status was within the general rubric of mining, which has a hierarchy of jobs of its own.

Radby is probably the nearest study in this country to the complex procedures employed by Warner in a small town in the United States, in which not only were the usual background data collected but each participant was asked to place himself in relation to other people in the town. There is a threefold classification of the working class in this study also.[16] In *Elmtown's Youth*,[17] another study of a small American town, there are five strata, but the two highest are very small. There is considerable preponderance of manual workers in the two bottom classes, and some of those in other classifications are proprietors of shops and similar places on various levels, and the 158 heads of households in the third of the five classes still contain 39 'craftsmen and machine operators', 20 'farm tenants' and 4 'service workers and labourers'.

The preponderance of smaller towns or restricted neighbourhoods in the more detailed samples is something of a problem because it tends to obscure the existence of a small class of families which, although not necessarily to be described as problem families in the social work sense, have very considerable problems and are so far removed from the normal standards of the working class, and produce so large a proportion of people who become the customers of social work services, that they must be considered as a deviant group. A number of those described in the two lowest groups in Radby fall into this group, and they obviously exist in the smaller towns, but they congregate in much greater numbers in the larger urban areas. On a restricted definition, Harriet Wilson found 157 of these families in Cardiff and there are probably quite a number on the borderline of her definition.[18] The deviant stratum is probably in the main a substratum of the lower working class (sometimes described as 'rough'), but may have a membership which extends outside the unskilled stratum.

In what follows I propose to speak in general, when not referring to occupations, to the *upper*, *middle*, *lower* and *deviant* strata, with the important provisos that these are only generally related to the skilled, semiskilled, unskilled classification and that the deviant stratum is mainly, but not entirely, a substratum of the lower; and remembering that particular studies tend to order their classifications in relation to the situation in the places they are studying, so that they are not entirely comparable.

Class consciousness and conflict

Much has been made of the opposition of interest between the manual and non-manual classes, in particular between employers and workers. Here we are not so much concerned with the possible effects upon society in general of assumptions concerning the differing strengths of class solidarity and conflict. Studies constantly report statements implying community of interest—'we're all working class here'—and feelings of opposition—'we're the ones who really do the work'; but it is doubtful if these indicate any very strong feelings of solidarity. The near equality of support enjoyed by the two major political parties in England is based upon the existence of many working-class Conservative supporters, often described as 'deferential' voters, and, as noted above, Lockwood has recently extended this concept to define a category who are neither detached from the older working class traditions nor militantly attached to the idea of working-class solidarity. While this probably implies a degree of passivity and acceptance of things as they are, both in work and non-work roles, it is doubtful if there is a wide range of social behaviour which distinguishes the 'deferential' group from others.

Opposition of interest is obviously most strongly expressed in work situations, where it is aided by unionisation, and especially where there are continuing grievances. Outside these situations, it is less well maintained, leadership being left to a few working-class activists and to middle-class vicars, teachers, councillors and the like. There are situations where a sense of grievance unite people to attain some specific end—making a main road safe to cross, providing schools or bus services—but these have little to do with class conflict in the classical sense. The general feeling tends to be, as Hoggart points out, that there is nothing one can do about 'Them', the officials, and it is better to put up with things as they are.

On the other hand, there is a form of working-class solidarity which is in some degree related to that which Marx and Engels would have liked to create; a sense of all being in the same boat, and of common suffering, much enlarged by the ties of living in the same neighbourhood for generations. More will be said about this in chapter 5.

General approach

In general, therefore, the view will be taken that there are a few major structural characteristics, primarily occupation, income, mobility and educational levels, which impose greater or less limitations, and imply similar action in other spheres of social behaviour. These in their turn are constrained by historical and structural factors which it would take us too far afield to discuss. The reactions to these are functional in the sense that they help to create a system of social relationships which provide a successful adaptation to the constraints imposed; but this does not assume general or total success in this aim. The working class has behind it generation on generation subject to extreme constraint, constituting a danger to existence; and severe restrictions on individual capacity to innovate or escape. It also forms part of a larger society, the conflicting values of which it distils in its own peculiar ways. Thus, partial solutions which are confused, uncertain, and even severely dysfunctional, are not surprising. A pretty pattern of interlocking relationships, rights and duties would be surprising in these circumstances.

For the most part what follows is a description of what is known about the working class, laying more emphasis upon variations between strata within that class, than upon general class consciousness or conflicts of interest with other classes. Much of the material is extremely vague about which part of the working class it is supposed to be describing; and where no other indication is given the reader is expected to take the view that what is said refers to the middle stratum, that is, to the main body of working-class people, and is less characteristic of the upper and lower.

The worker at work

Since much of the time of men, and increasingly of women, is spent at work, we need to look at some of the characteristics of manual work, and the experience and problems of the workers at work.

It is something of a stereotype that in contrast to the middle class, working-class men achieve a level of occupational status and wages quite quickly and then stay there. The recent Labour Mobility Survey makes it clear that this is not true of a substantial proportion of the manual labour force. Job changing is frequent and often leads to changes in status. Over ten years to 1963 the most usual length of employment in a job for men in skilled manual jobs was two years (17 per cent). However, 70 per cent of the jobs held by unskilled men lasted less than one year (the corresponding figure for non-manual partly skilled was 62 per cent). Redundancy is increasingly a reason as we move from skilled to unskilled, but even in the unskilled, it accounted for only 20 per cent of the moves; while getting a better job accounted for another 16 per cent. The major reason given was dislike of the work, or something connected with it—skilled 27 per cent; partly skilled 28 per cent; unskilled 38 per cent (the number saying they were sacked was low, and it is impossible to know if this is misinformation). Almost half of the job changes made by the unskilled led to higher job status; but only 44 per cent of the changes led to higher pay, a lower proportion than in the partly skilled (51 per cent) and skilled (54 per cent).

Since there is comparatively little long range geographical movement, this means that there is a considerable amount of changing jobs in a particular area. There seems to have been little change in occupational status with one employer so that the major pattern is to change jobs in order to find something you like better, or to

24

obtain advancement or better pay. As time goes on there is, of course, a tendency to settle into one job, and it seems that a man who has been in a job six years is much more likely to stay. Firms try to encourage this by pension schemes, and other incentives.

The very highly paid jobs, for example in the motor vehicle industry, attract a particular type of married man who has a strong attachment to money and is prepared to move a long way and, if necessary, to give up his skilled status and work on an assembly line in order to get it. Part of the unskilled force is also highly mobile in search of money, but this is a comparatively small minority.

Job satisfaction

Much of the commitment of the worker to his job depends on the satisfactions he derives from it. These can best be discussed under three broad headings: those relating to the nature of the job itself, those relating to the formal organisation within which he is working and those relating to the informal organisation.

The skilled worker is most likely to derive satisfaction directly from the work he is doing, although much may depend upon the degree to which advancing technology curtails the range within which he can use his skills, or threatens his range of skills altogether. At any time there are a range of skills which are declining, while the demand for others is increasing, and the speed of these changes has been accelerating in recent years.

Limitations upon satisfactions are often assessed partly in terms of independence of action, partly in terms of the general status of the craft in relation to others. As one moves down the scale repetition becomes a feature of the work, but many unskilled jobs have a degree of variety and also some independence of action. Labouring takes a variety of forms, and is often without the pressure of the factory floor; the hospital porter may do a great many different things in different places with different people.

Even in the extremely repetitive type of factory work, it is easy for the middle-class observer to overemphasise the tedium factor. Baldamus[1] draws attention to an antidote to tedium, what he calls 'traction', consisting in various features in the process itself, which give satisfaction: completing a run or a certain number of articles, the rhythm of a series of repeated movements performed with ease and rapidity, or keeping up with an assembly line. Payment by results obviously helps, but there may be much pleasure in actually doing the job; just as the labourer may enjoy the physical pleasure of digging, lifting or carrying, and indeed feel superior to those weedy weaklings shut up in the factory. Increasing production, or any general feeling of improvement, may also aid this effect, as was ably demonstrated in one of the experiments in that classic of industrial investigation, the Hawthorne project.[2]

Jobs may be dirty, hot, hard, noisy or otherwise unpleasant. While there is often pride in accomplishment in those who do them, they are often also disliked by many workers, so that a particular shop may be rejected by the rest of the factory, and its workers accorded lower status whatever their formal skill position. High wages compensate for this to some extent, but they tend to lead to a self-selection of the workers who are prepared to take this view of them.

The nature of the work process obviously has an important effect on the formal organisation of the workshop, the skill and pay structure, and the form of supervision, although it is by no means definitive even at shop floor level. The processes may throw up small groups or larger groups, working as teams or working independently, and may control the ease of communication between one worker and another. (This can be overcome; in weaving shops where noise level often seems high to visitors, and supervision of a number of looms may appear to separate the workers, the women nevertheless appear to chat fairly easily.)

Pay structures are immensely variable and complex, and the effects of national negotiations are often extremely difficult to determine because of the variability of local arrangements. As has already been said, the possibility of changing jobs to get more pay is considerable in the larger urban areas, but progressively restricted as the variety and range of industry is limited where the worker lives. Thus in areas with a limited choice, the worker may be faced with a prospect of considerable upheaval, involving his family, if he wants to improve his position; furthermore, unlike the non-manual worker who is likely to be on an ascending scale, he much more often has to contemplate a change in the whole job situation in order to get better pay; and even where investment in the work itself is less high, other job satisfactions tend to bulk large. The manual worker is thus heavily exposed to cross pressures between family and work, probably as heavily in the early family years as the professional, who less often has to contend with his own strong kinship ties and an immobile wife.

The supervisory structure also plays a considerable part in the question of job satisfaction. The natural groupings which result from the process often, in themselves, give rise to close supervision, or more distant authority, but management decisions here play a considerable role. Amongst the men there tend to be strong feelings of independence and autonomy and this makes the role of the foreman somewhat uneasy as he is caught up in management decisions which may well have been taken without consulting him, and which may not be appropriate, or if appropriate, may not be popular; while he cannot be too authoritarian or distant if he is to remain in control. In some industries, notably engineering, he also has to contend with the shop steward, who can be used as an additional form of pressure, or another channel to management. The success with which he deals with these cross currents may have considerable effect upon the satisfaction the individual worker derives from the job situation.

We now turn to some aspects of the informal organisation. The size of the work group has already been mentioned, but the nature of the group is obviously vital. Some men prefer to remain apart from groupings, and they may choose more independent jobs. For the most part, however, work is done in some kind of group, even if this consists, as on the buses, of two-man teams. An enormous amount of research has been directed to the nature of work groups, but like most research on face-to-face groups, the results are diverse, and exceptionally difficult to summarise. What is said here very largely follows the analysis by Fogarty, and by Miller and Form,[3] whose books are likely to be available to the student for further consultation.

Within any group, face-to-face or larger, there is a balance of ascribed and achieved roles. The ascribed roles roughly follow the skill hierarchy but particularise much more in terms of the actual job being done. Whyte's analysis of ascribed status in the restaurant industry is often quoted; and demonstrates a distinct hierarchy amongst food preparers from salad to fish.[4] Ascribed status in work performed may, however, conflict with other types of ascribed status, e.g. age, sex, or with achieved status dependent upon personality, length of service, marital status, or other factors. Because of this the internal status positions in the group may be upset by changes in constitution or membership, and these may increase or decrease job satisfactions for other workers.

Race and ethnic groupings are less of a problem in Britain than in some other countries, but where they exist they may affect the constitution of groups, status within groups, or the relative status of groups as a whole. Small, and particularly interdependent working groups tend to be highly exclusive, but the larger groups may also exhibit strong prejudices. Sheila Patterson records the strength of workshop feeling against coloured workers in some firms in London, but also notes some situations in which they have been found acceptable.[5]

The working group often has very strong views on what is proper conduct for its members. Craft groups have distinct standards about working clothes, maintenance of tools, and cleanliness; but other groups may also have standards of this kind which are sometimes opposite, for example old work clothes, not being afraid of getting yourself dirty. Work groups also tend to have strong views about the amount of work a member should do, and this can influence production of the whole group and completely defeat group bonus schemes. The most famous example of this is the bank wiring room in the Hawthorne study. This particular group code also served another function, of protection against interlopers, since they kept their production limitations to themselves, and avoided any 'squealing' to the supervisor.

This is only one type of group. Some reinforce each other in maintaining high work or production standards, some in strong opposition to management. It must also be remembered that many work groups have no strong solidarity, though they have some feelings of common interest, and under pressure may easily break up into cliques.

The work group often not only has strongly sanctioned norms, but also has customs, conventions, and a kind of folklore. There are approved permanent jokes—about Joe who has acquired the reputation of being a bit of a boy with the girls, or Harry who is always complaining about his mother-in-law (note how these situations which easily come to mind are reinforcements of standard working-class jokes). There are often very strong conventions about the joking relationships between men and women, conventions which are extremely subtle, and bring down immense wrath upon the head of anyone overstepping the mark, even though to the outside observer, acceptable repartee may well appear extremely rude and crude. In men's groups there are conventions about sex talk and swearing; while it may be customary to interlace one's remarks at almost every other word with expletives long since detached from their original sexual connotations, the man who makes a crude remark about his wife or his mother is likely to find himself regarded as a 'foul mouthed bastard' and treated with great distaste.

Groups also support weak members and younger members (despite conventional induction rites), and prevent injustice and hurt pride. Working groups can be overwhelmingly kind and helpful, especially to any member who is in trouble. They can also be spiteful, prejudiced and bitterly destructive against people they do not accept.

The work group is, therefore, very much a small society, which can offer many satisfactions apart from interest in work, or money earned. One of the major reasons for the popularity of work amongst married women is the working atmosphere where they can gossip, discuss their insides, sing, and enjoy all the pleasures of doorstep living—and get paid for it.

It is obvious that the work group reproduces at many points the outside culture; its status system, its values, and its interests. The work-centred, single firm community most strongly demonstrates

29

this overlap, but it is present in any work situation. The informal group also acts as a communications centre, as do the working men's clubs. Within the works the informal grapevine passes round information, misinformation and rumour with great rapidity. Women may have reputations as gossips, but gossip by men at work, about work, about sport, or other matters, is just as intensive and all-pervading.

Women at work

As is well known, the proportion of women working has been rising rapidly in the 1950s and 1960s. This is partly a recovery from a very low proportion in the interwar period, but it primarily represents a new situation in which though marriage rates are high, family planning is widespread and labour shortage is a permanent feature of an overextended economy. The rise covers both full and part-time employment. In terms of skill, the opportunities for women have lessened, partly because of the decline of the textile and clothing industries, and mainly because of the considerable increase in married as against single women, since the former more often tend to take semiskilled or unskilled jobs. Just over one-third of semiskilled and unskilled manual workers in 1963 were female, but only one-eighth of skilled manual workers. The growth of service industries has tended to divert women into non-manual jobs, and the 1963 Labour Mobility Survey shows that nearly 60 per cent of skilled non-manual and just over 70 per cent of semiskilled non-manual workers were women. Most of the increase has been in older married women. Thus, the average age of the female labour force has risen, and the proportion in part-time work has also increased. Although the increasing marriage rate takes a greater number of women out of the labour market for some period, and in the twenty to twenty-four age group the proportion of married women working is expected to decline from 39 per cent in 1966 to 35 per cent in 1971 and then stay there; for ages over thirty-five the proportion will rise steadily and will be over 50 per cent by 1981, and for the age group forty to fifty-four will be nearly 60 per cent.[6]

Some information about the effect of this at different levels in the working class can be seen in a table in the 1961 Census which shows the proportion of wives working.[7] Where the husband himself is working, this declines from 35 per cent in skilled manual workers to 31·5 per cent in the unskilled. When the husband is not working, it rises from 4·6 per cent to 6·1 per cent. Where they have children, the unskilled figure (26·2 per cent) is lower than the skilled (27 per cent) but the semiskilled are higher than both (28 per cent). This no doubt reflects a complex relationship between the increase in mean family size as one moves downward, and variations in age of wife and of children. It should be noted that the proportion of working husbands with wives at work is highest among junior non-manual workers (36 per cent), and also high among intermediate non-manual workers (34·4 per cent); both of these groups are also high on the proportion of working wives with children. Some of the studies show that the better the educational background, the more likely it is that wives will work, but these comparisons have been heavily affected by the inclusion of professional women. Probably the most important factor governing the willingness of a woman to work is whether she has a child under five, and this outweighs other considerations, and no doubt largely accounts for the lower rate of working wives amongst the unskilled where mean family size is greater.

Since marriage rates are rising, and the age of the wife declining, it is likely that the stage of being free of care of a child under five is likely to be reached earlier. It is probable that there will be continuing increases in the number of married women working who are in their late twenties or early thirties. The possible effects on husband–wife roles are discussed in later chapters.

Trade unions

Possibly because he first discovered it, the British working man has very strong beliefs in solidarity and common action. This may not be very apparent in the degree of support he gives to union activities but it is there, and is likely to reveal itself if there is any serious dispute. The question of solidarity may be related to a background of complex interrelationships outside the works; but is more commonly seen in the strong communal feeling of many work groups, which react immediately to a fancied injustice to a member, and which are very sensitive to the background noise of rumours always circulating in a factory. Strikes are rarely primarily about money these days, they are usually about justice, or insecurity, or both.

In 1965 in the Jaguar factory there was an argument about the polishing of some door frames, involving two workmen. The foreman wanted them redone and the workmen said they were already flawed and asked for extra money. The usual procedure of calling in the floor superintendent and the shop steward led to no agreement; the polishing shop then came out on strike. This sort of thing happens constantly. In this particular case the management stuck its heels in, the men were equally obdurate and the whole works eventually stopped because of the interruption in the work flow. Suppliers were also affected. The strike lasted a month, and cost the firm an estimated £4 million in output.

As in so many strikes of this kind, it is exceedingly difficult to say what it was about. There was a pay issue; there was an issue of just treatment; there was a Communist shop steward involved; there was irrationality and obstinacy on both sides; it was summer and just before Whitsun when the strike started; the car industry had been suffering from a good deal of fluctuation in recent years—no doubt all of these things had something to do with it. Strikes of this kind very often appear to be the unintended consequences of a situation in which the two sides have managed to get themselves into a position where their honour is involved.

Strikes are, however, a comparatively minor outcrop of a vast amount of negotiation, and settlement of grievances and disputes, mainly at shop floor level. The union is for the most part a kind of appeal machinery which oils frictions. Its second function so far as the individual worker is concerned is to see that he keeps up in the steady progress of pay increases and improvement of hours and conditions. In this the unions are caught in a vice, of which one jaw is the agreed need for the restraint of wage and cost inflation, as embodied in the Government's prices and incomes policy, and the other is the need to keep their members happy by seeing that they keep up, even if others do not.

The situation is exacerbated by the age and creaking complexity of the union system. In 1965 there were no less than 580 unions in the United Kingdom, the great majority of them very small. Some 70 per cent of the membership is in some ten large unions, of which the largest are the Transport and General Workers' Union and the Amalgamated Engineering Union. Six of these (including these two) are growing, two static and two declining. These last (the National Union of Mineworkers and National Union of Railwaymen) are, in H. A. Turner's phrase, 'closed' unions,[8] that is unions in which the potential membership is restricted, often by the fact that they are devoted to a particular industry or occupation. Their decline is obviously the result of basic changes in the position of the coal and railway industries. Most of the others are 'open' unions who are prepared to take in a widening range of trades and occupations. There is some movement towards structures which take under one umbrella a range of different groups, such as the TGWU, and thus tend to reduce demarcation problems, while deploying great reserves of strength, if necessary. There is currently (1967) a Royal Commission considering these and other problems (its papers are a useful source of information).

The significance of all this for the working class is considerable. The gradual concentration of power makes it possible to act with strength, and may help simplify some of the more unwanted inter-union aspects in disputes. It also presents the worker, in an acute form, with the conflict between individual and joint rights and responsibilities. No large union can be totally unresponsive to a demand from the Government to follow its economic policies, and these are increasingly in terms of restraints. How is this to be translated into the friendly, loyal atmosphere of the work groups? for if this is not done unofficial strikes will rise alarmingly. And if they do, conflicts between the needs of work and non-work roles is likely to increase also.

Some of the changes going on in the traditional working class are tending to lead to a greater accent on money and possessions. It might well be asked whether the extreme case of craftsmen working on an assembly line in the motor industry merely for higher pay, will spread to other industries. If there is more satisfaction in home and leisure, will work satisfaction decline, and the union become progressively a way of putting up earnings, both on specific jobs and nationally? Goldthorpe and Lockwood[9] have argued that there is a convergence in attitudes to unions in the middle and working classes, in both cases centred around bettering pay and conditions for the individual, with little sense of class solidarity or interest in political action, or anything else a union might provide; that is unionisation as an instrument rather than an end in itself. If so, the move is much more on the non-manual side, but it is probably true that the last bastions of union-centred living are crumbling with the types and conditions of work which gave rise to them, and with the widening horizons of the manual worker.

Income, education, health, housing

In previous chapters we have looked in some detail at occupational factors. We now come to a number of other major influences moulding working class life: income (and lack of it), education, health, and housing.

It is perhaps necessary to point out that there is no specific section on unemployment, which would have loomed large in any book of this kind before World War II. Unemployment remains a shadow on the horizon, but we are now used to such low levels that even a rise to $2\frac{1}{2}$ per cent is followed by a public outcry. It is certainly true that unemployment for any length of time is a very bad thing for those that experience it, and those who protest are fundamentally right in doing so. We have not apparently discovered how to release the pressures on the British economy without a rise in unemployment, nor have we faced the need to provide adequate income for the comparative few who are affected. Nevertheless unemployment now is largely a temporary period of poverty, and can well be treated under that heading.

Income

It is difficult to say to what degree and in what way prestige attaches to income in the working class. There are undoubtedly considerable overlaps between the ranges of earnings between different occupational strata and different industries, although average earnings can be seen to fall as one moves down the scale. It may be that hourly and weekly wage rates are more often regarded as forming a prestige hierarchy than actual earnings—certainly much trade union negotiation goes on in these terms, often with the strongest possible accent on differentials.

The earnings of the head of the household may also form a hierarchy of this kind, but may contribute more strongly to a hierarchy
of possessions and leisure spending. The actual household income
varies considerably, depending upon the number of earners; and the
disposable income is different again since this takes into account tax
deductions. A more precise statement would include offsets for
direct benefits paid by the state, for example family allowances and
other social security benefits, and cheap school meals. An indirect
but extremely important benefit is rent control and regulation, and
subsidised (and often means tested) council housing.

Routh[1] suggests that pay differentials tend to widen when prices
are stable or slowly rising, as in the periods 1944–50 and 1956–60,
and to narrow when inflation is proceeding more rapidly. This derives from a feeling in periods of rapid price rises that lower paid
workers should benefit more; and also from the type of increase
claimed. Since 1913, however, the differentials in the manual grades
have remained fairly constant, although the greater rigidity of salaries
and changes in the nature of clerical work has led to a considerable
narrowing of the gap between manual and non-manual. Lockwood
has examined this relationship at length and shows that clerical
workers began to lose ground in the late 1930s, and by the mid-50s,
the major proportion of clerks were earning at about the same rate
as the average manual worker. (Ministry of Labour figures[2] for recent
years show for all manufacturing industries very similar average
earnings (not rates) for both men and women, comparing all weekly
paid manual workers with weekly paid workers in administrative,
technical and clerical grades.) Routh finds that between 1906 and
1960 there has been a widening of the range in the top half of the
distribution of male manual earnings, but the dispersion in the
bottom half has been constant since 1938 at least. Between 1938 and
1960 there was some narrowing of the differential between men and
women, but women's wages remain substantially lower than men's.
Ministry of Labour figures for average weekly earnings for 1959–66
show the women's average to be just under half the men's. If we look
at the figures in terms of skill classes, we find that for males over
the whole period 1913–14 to 1960, unskilled workers have done a

little better than semiskilled. Between 1955–56 and 1960 however, the skilled were improving their average earnings slightly more than the other two classes, who were gaining at about the same rate.

There has recently been a good deal of argument as to whether there really has been a substantial downward redistribution of income since 1938. Lydall and Paish[3] both concluded that there was, but recently Titmuss[4] has produced a detailed criticism of the figures upon which their conclusions were based, and raised considerable doubts about the validity of their results. It seems likely that the criticism which has been levelled at US studies in the same field is also true here; that too much emphasis is placed upon the reduction in the share in the national income of a small proportion of incomes at the top end of the distribution, without paying enough attention to the question of who benefited, who are not those with the lowest incomes.[5] Prest and Stark[6] have recently used a more sophisticated method of assessing change in the degree of redistribution for the period 1949–63, and find a trend towards greater equality; they comment that this is probably understated because of the shortness of the period. The question whether income differentials have narrowed in comparison with the prewar data is probably now unanswerable, but it seems likely that they were doing so in the 1950s and early 1960s.

Although the Ministry of Labour's Family Expenditure Surveys are now providing some information about household income and a good deal about expenditure, and further information can be got from the returns of the Board of Inland Revenue and other sources, it is extremely difficult to relate this to any measure of stratification, especially as the large number of retired small households with very small incomes distort the figures. What is clear, however, is that the smaller the income, the greater the importance of supplementation from the wife's earnings (this is a feature of the latest poverty study, mentioned below). Furthermore, the different levels of rates and rents, varied by the existence of rate rebate schemes, or controlled or regulated under the Rent Act 1965, are increasingly issues of importance in working-class budgets.

Poverty

This brings us to the subject of poverty. The measurement of poverty is essentially relative since any line one draws, whether it is of income, or in terms of nutrition and other necessities, is dependent on judgment. There is, of course, a basic amount of food without which starvation ensues, but even this may vary according to the levels to which the growing child has been trained. There can be much disagreement about minimum levels in our society, and the attempt to turn this into a costed budget is always hazardous.

The tendency has been to work on the basis of some low standard of human needs, as in the Rowntree classics. More recent studies have been related to the national assistance (now supplementary benefit) levels, which are themselves remotely related to Rowntree. The two first Rowntree studies (1899 and 1936) brought out the continuing importance of low earnings and large families. The third study (1950) is less carefully carried out but pointed more strongly to the effect of old age.

The recent analysis of data from the Ministry of Labour 1953–4 and 1960 Family Expenditure Surveys by Abel-Smith and Townsend[7] was intended rather to open up the subject than to give accurate figures, since the data are somewhat deficient and not altogether comparable. The broad conclusions are probably correct enough: that there had been an increase in the number of people living below the level of 40 per cent above the National Assistance standard (itself doubtfully at subsistence level). The results for 1960, which are more reliable, show 17·9 per cent of households, and 14·2 per cent of persons in them (about $7\frac{1}{2}$ million) below the 140 per cent level; and 4·7 per cent and 3·8 per cent (2 m) below the basic assistance scale. the authors estimate that about 3 m of the 7 m were over pensionable age and that about $2\frac{1}{4}$ m children were included in the total.

The publication of this report led to a Ministry enquiry[8] consisting of a random sample of 2,600 families receiving family allowances. This study, carried out in 1966, shows that of the total of 3·9 m families with two or more children, some 280,000 fell below the national assistance scales in that year. These families included

910,000 children. Of these about 135,000 families with 400,000 children were receiving national assistance, covering 90 per cent of the fatherless families; 81 per cent of those where the father was sick or unemployed for more than three months; 48 per cent of all types. National assistance could not be applied to those in work or given in full where the wage stop was operated, and these two categories represented some 85,000 families; while 75,000 families appeared to be eligible for assistance and were not getting it. Since then new supplementary benefit scales have been introduced and the basic levels have risen, thus the number below them has risen also; but the proportion receiving the benefit has also risen, at the time of writing to an unknown extent. It is estimated that the number of families of all types, including those with one child, who were below supplementary benefit standard and could not be brought up to it because the fathers were in full-time work or wage-stopped (mainly the former) was 160,000, including about half a million children. This is an unwelcome reminder that in the affluent society there is still a substantial proportion who cannot earn enough to keep themselves out of poverty.

There are several classes of people who are primarily affected. First of all and best known, there are those whose income is entirely or almost entirely restricted to state benefits; the most obvious class is that of old people, although there are also the handicapped, mentally and physically, including the long-term mentally ill not in institutions. Secondly, there are those with large families who are in full-time work and earning too little to provide adequately for their families; and those who are 'available for work', but often only for light work, but are 'wage-stopped' (a protection for public funds, based upon the same assumption as the Poor Law Amendment Act 1834; that large numbers would draw public money unless they were prevented; this was a valid assumption in 1834). The third class contains that part of the fatherless families where the mother is unsupported from other sources, and either cannot both earn and look after the child, or can only earn on low women's wages.

A large-scale survey is in progress at the time of writing, covering large families, the long-term sick, and fatherless families. A good deal more information will be available from this, but it is likely that a substantial number of people, including many children, are still in primary poverty—they do not have enough to eat; and many more in secondary poverty—they can only get enough to eat if they are particularly good managers and live lives deprived of practically everything else.

Education

It is now so well established that the children of manual workers are less well served by, and less successful than, middle-class children of equal ability throughout most of the educational system, that there is hardly any point in assembling the evidence here, although some relevant points will be discussed. The evidence is to be found in Crowther, Plowden, Newsom and Robbins, and in Douglas, and Floud, Halsey and Martin.[9] Similar evidence concerning nursery education is produced by Deutsch.[10] The general tenor of these studies is that the children of manual workers are less well motivated and academically oriented, so that they obtain a limited benefit at each stage; and very much fewer than their abilities would indicate reach higher education. Nevertheless the children of manual workers who do enter universities do as well as middle-class children.

More manual than non-manual workers also have larger families, and children from larger families show lower intelligence test scores than those from smaller families and do less well at school. This applies throughout the strata but in middle-class families the effect only shows in families of four or more, while in the working class it is more obvious with every increase in family size. A number of studies support the view that children in large families in general tend to get rather less care, especially where they are not well spaced, and Douglas suggests, from evidence provided by health visitors and schools, that this is due to a generally poorer standard of maternal care in large working-class families; although he also shows that these deficiencies appear to have their major effect in early life, and certainly before his eight-year-olds were tested.

It is also clear that parental aspirations are of considerable importance. Jackson and Marsden[11] distinguish between working-class parents who clearly encourage their children to succeed, and those who do not; and much of Douglas's analysis is based on responses indicating the educational aspirations of the mother. A factor analysis reported in Vol. 2 of Plowden brings out parental attitudes as accounting for more of the variation in school achievement than home circumstances (covering a number of things indicating income, occupation, education and neighbourhood status of the parents), or than a measure of the variation in educational standards in the schools concerned. The most important factor in the school situation was the quality of teaching. While these results show what might be expected from other studies, they should be treated with great caution. The factors extracted leave unexplained a substantial proportion of the variation, and are themselves based upon interpretations about which there could be considerable disagreement, of answers to a number of questions. The criterion of achievement used is a reading comprehension test, which also might be regarded as somewhat limited.

There is obviously room for a lot more study of precisely what it is that governs the reaction of the child to teaching. Parental approval is obviously of importance to the child but it can be expressed in a number of ways ranging from 'you carry on, it's all right with me' to 'if you don't do better at school, I'll beat the living daylights out of you'. Since there are two parents and often older siblings with whom the child is emotionally identified, the possible combinations of these attitudes and variations in the emotional atmosphere are large.

On the school side the attitude of the staff is equally complex. Recently Lacey and Hargreaves[12] have each shown in relation to a heavily working-class comprehensive secondary school, how the attitudes of the staff tend to crystallise the attitudes of boys to the school so that after an initial period of settling in, a pro-school, academically successful and approved series of groupings arise in the higher streams; while anti-school, low academic success, disapproved groups take possession of the lower streams. These groups then

4

interact with staff attitudes so that the better ones get better and the worse get worse. Conformity in the pro-school groupings supports the work and good conduct ethic; conformity in the anti-school groupings is strongly and violently opposed to it, to such an extent that by the fourth form the teachers concerned have given up and connive at cheating in order to live a quiet life.

It is obviously difficult for teachers who are themselves strongly dependent on academic success throughout their training, working in a system which values academic success and increasingly uses it as a basis for admission to well paid and high status work, to avoid a system of values which gives it priority in the school. It is difficult for headmasters to avoid giving the 'best' classes to the 'best' teachers; or to prevent the drift of staff away from aged schools filled with uninterested children, to new schools with rather more interested children. The problem of how to educate the unmotivated is not a matter for discussion here. The need for the essentially conforming and middle-class teacher to understand the mode of life, and the thought processes of the working-class child, and particularly the lower-working-class child, is great, but it is only the beginning of the ability to handle his education.

Health : Physical

In this and the following section we deal with disease and disorders in general, but more specific comments are made in later sections on child-rearing and old people.

Poverty, poor housing which makes hygiene difficult to maintain, and overcrowding, have always been associated with disease in the minds of most people. To a considerable extent the gradients of mortality and morbidity from various types of disease bear this out, but there are a number of diseases where the gradients are reversed. Coronary heart disease is a case in point. As Susser and Watson[13] point out, the increase in the last half century is so sharp that this disease is assuming epidemic proportions amongst middle- and upper-class middle-aged men. The disease has a high incidence in the richer countries and seems to be associated with a particular way of life, as studies of immigrants have shown. It appears to be particularly closely associated with sedentary occupations, and manual work is probably some protection against it, though there are other factors also.

Poliomyelitis is also more prevalent in the middle classes. It is suggested that this is due to general low-grade infection in crowded conditions which produces antibodies and protects against more serious infection, but it is not clear why this works so much better for polio than for other infectious diseases.

For the most part, however, mortality and morbidity rates increase steadily as we move down the scale, not only between non-manual and manual workers, but category by category; and the relative positions in 1930–32 and 1950 are much the same. The Registrar-General's Class V for instance, shows much higher mortality in males aged twenty to sixty-four for cancer of the stomach, rheumatic heart disease (but the differences in children are much smaller and this may disappear) and chronic bronchitis, than for Class I; and the rates are distinctly higher than for Classes IV and III. Bronchitis is probably due initially to infection, but this is maintained and aggravated by various environmental agents, of which the best known are smoking; air pollution, both in the atmosphere and in industry; and dust, draughts and extremes of temperature at work.[14] The labourer is more likely to be exposed to a combination of these conditions than any other category, and he may be less likely to go for early treatment. Manual workers in general are, to a lesser degree, in the same situation.

That the situation is probably more complex than this is demonstrated by studies of infant mortality.[15] The gradient between 1911 and 1950 has been strongly downwards in all classes, but the relationship between them has remained virtually the same, indeed the gap between Class I and IV is even a little higher. The biggest changes are to be found in post-neonatal deaths (four weeks to one year) and here the non-manual Class II seems to have added to its advantage and pulled away from the skilled manual Class III. If, however, we look at miners, whether graded as III or IV, the infant mortality rates are higher than Class V (unskilled) throughout, and in 1939

Class III miners had higher rates than Class IV although the gap subsequently closed.

In a study of mortality and morbidity from cancer in North Wales and Liverpool, Stocks found a number of significant differences in the standardised rates for different areas which are difficult to explain, although some of them seem related to frequent beer drinking. There is no indication of whether or not social class differences are of any importance.[16]

Some information about morbidity is available as a result of an analysis carried out by W. P. D. Logan of some 280,000 clinical records from over 100 general practitioners in England and Wales.[17] These show for adult males, a gradient of increasing frequency of consultations from Class I to V in over half of the disease groups considered. Bronchitis shows the clearest and steepest gradient, thus following the mortality figures, but coronary artery disease shows no gradient. Diabetes is also higher in the middle class. Tuberculosis shows no gradient but this result is much affected by special hospital out-patient services, as indeed are a number of the other diseases to a lesser extent. Mineworkers again come out as subject to particularly high rates in a number of diseases. With some changes, the picture is similar for women. The evidence also suggests that while in a number of categories incidence is higher in Class V, in others incidence is not greatly different but severity is greater, and in some cases both.

A suggestion put forward is that there may be a cultural lag in the deployment of rising incomes, in health knowledge and in the use of medical services. There has been a slow narrowing of the gap between income groups in the height of children and it may be that this indicates that the manual workers are catching up. Another suggestion is that a process of human sorting is going on, and that therefore not only the least intelligent but also the weediest are falling to the bottom. As we have seen, there is a considerable amount of social mobility upwards and downwards. There is no evidence in the studies yet made that the amount of mobility has changed over the various cohorts, but this may be compounded of all sorts of factors and the mix may be moving towards a selection on quality. There is some evidence for this in an Aberdeen study of women with their first babies. Those who have married 'downwards' tend to have higher 'obstetric' death rates and a higher proportion of prematures than those who stay where they are or move upward. Furthermore, those who marry downwards are physically smaller (and therefore more likely to have babies of small size, under the prematurity weight level, where there is a higher perinatal risk) and they are also of lower intelligence; and the converse is true of those who marry upwards (see 13).

It is probable also that the utilisation of services varies between classes. The middle classes get the most out of the National Health Service by utilising it intelligently and they are probably less likely to resort to traditional remedies, or to use a network of kinship and friendship consultation before taking the case to the doctor. The greater ease in communication of the middle classes also makes it easier for them to talk to doctors—in the next section we shall see how important this is in the use of talking therapies. A stronger tradition of endurance, combined with the more immediate impact of loss of pay, are also strong deterrents for the working class.

Cartwright,[18] in a large-scale study of patients in hospital, found that working-class patients were less willing to complain or even ask for information, and that these tendencies were strongest in Social Class V. They tended more often to obtain information about illness from nurses rather than doctors, and from other patients, whose company they enjoyed more than did the middle-class people. While in hospital they were more likely to obtain help from relatives to look after families at home. In general, the hospitals came out of this enquiry well, showing no discrimination in the standards of care; and general satisfaction was expressed by patients.

Studies carried out in Scotland, following up hospital patients, show the considerable disadvantages experienced, particularly by the unskilled worker, both in poor housing and even more in the difficulty of not being able to move into a job suitable to the patient's state of health (although this seems to be largely a product of unemployment in the areas concerned), but in the Dundee study an analysis of subsequent medical progress showed that it was Social Class II who did worst, mainly due to non-attendance for therapy.[19]

Health: Mental Illness

Difficulties in diagnosis make it hazardous to discuss the distribution of the mentally ill in the population. Admissions to hospitals show rates considerably lower than field surveys, and cannot be taken as a guide, and in any case the trend is away from hospital treatment. The field surveys are more likely to find cases, but it is difficult to carry them out on a large enough scale.

Studies of the distribution of psychosis indicate that it is more heavily concentrated in the working class and particularly the lower stratum.[20] A good deal of work has been done on schizophrenia in particular, and the rate per 100,000 in Class V is double that in Class IV; but equally the rates in Classes III and IV are double those in Classes I and II. These rates are based on hospital admissions. The gradient is less emphatic for manic-depressive psychosis.

A number of studies have been directed to the question whether schizophrenics are concentrated in Class V because they come from there, or whether they have moved downwards because of their illness. The conclusion seems to be that the latter is true and that this happens as the disease develops.[21]

The data on neurotics is much more uncertain but it seems likely that middle-class neurotics are more often seen in general practice, while they turn up as hospital admissions in the working class. It is not really possible to say whether the rates are actually higher in one class or the other.

In mental disorders, stress is often a considerable factor both in leading to the onset of a psychosis (and there is a distinct hereditary factor in psychoses), and in prolonging the illness or producing a recurrence. There is no very clear evidence about variations in strata on this, but it is very likely that the lower stratum contains a much greater likelihood of stress. On the other hand, entire failure of kinship support may well lead to long periods of institutionalisation, and the danger of this is higher in the lower stratum.

The situation is complex because of the difficulties which families experience in dealing with mental illness. The tendency is to treat even quite considerable aberrations as 'nerves' and to deal with them within the family. If, however, the actual behaviour of the person concerned becomes intolerable at home, or even worse, extremely visible, it is no longer possible to avoid calling in the authorities and recognising the presence of mental illness, particularly if hospitalisation ensues. The considerable increase of out-patient and general hospital treatment, particularly for depression, and the obvious rapid success of much of this treatment, has taken much of the fear and disgrace out of the situation, but it nevertheless remains a threat both to the family and to one's respectability to have to admit mental illness in the family.

It is clear from several American studies[22] that the contact between psychiatrists and working-class patients is poor. This is partly general dislike and fear of insanity, but it is also due to lack of familiarity in the working class with talking as a method of dealing with problems. Chemotherapy and physical treatments are much more acceptable, and the very considerable successes in these fields, particularly in the former in more recent years, make the process much easier. In illnesses which do not respond to these forms of treatment, some success has been achieved by creating group situations, especially within a therapeutic community as at the Henderson Hospital.[23] As in schizophrenia, however, most psychopathic states of any severity are still beyond our capacities in the treatment field, and both in the hospital system and in the prison system, we have so far failed to make any adequate arrangements, institutional or non-institutional to begin to deal with them successfully.

Health: Mental Subnormality

Severe subnormality is mainly due to heredity or to adverse conditions in pregnancy and birth. Mongolism is due to a genetic malfunction and shows itself more often in children born to older women. The survival rate of mongols has been increasing recently, largely due to better medical care, and the prevalence rates have therefore increased in the last thirty years. On the other hand, the prevalence rate of other forms of idiocy and imbecility has declined by about a third in this period.[24] This has probably been brought about by better nutrition, better antenatal and obstetric services, and better medical care in general. Since this is more easily available to the middle than working class, it is possible that the incidence of defects other than mongolism may show some class bias. In general, however, the incidence of idiocy and imbecility is not class based.

On the other hand feeblemindedness which represents the great majority of the subnormal population does seem to have a distinct cultural factor. Stein and Susser[25] found that children with brain damage are found equally in all social classes, but those without damage almost exclusively in those who belong to the manual strata. They therefore argue that there is a cultural syndrome of mental retardation which accounts for at least 75 per cent of the educationally subnormal and is, in principle, preventable.

As might be expected, the hospital population has a higher proportion of idiots and imbeciles and this is likely to become more pronounced as community services improve. Great Britain now has by far the best system of training centres for the severely subnormal who are living at home; built up by local authority health departments, despite the severe building restrictions, since 1945. The system covers virtually all those between six and sixteen and an increasing number of adults, and is being extended in the form of special care units to those who are both severely handicapped and severely subnormal, or too young for the junior traning centres. Local authorities have also had responsibility since 1913 for visiting and caring for the severely subnormal; and as education authorities, had some responsibility even before then.

The position regarding the educationally subnormal who remain within the educational system is probably less good. In January 1954 there were nearly 41,400 pupils in E.S.N. schools, and the total number ascertained was 51,800. A Government Committee suggested in 1929 that provision needed to be made for 1·2 per cent of all children at school, which would give a figure of 92,500, and experts might now set the figure higher. Those not in E.S.N. schools are probably in the bottom streams of schools, and many of these have some special teaching, but since they are concentrated in working-class areas which are in any case educationally underprivileged in every possible way, it is very doubtful indeed if they get the attention and special teaching they really need.

Housing

Housing the working class was first fully recognised as a public responsibility after World War I, although permissive powers to build had existed previously. The postwar government started off with rather higher standards than pre-1914, but with a backlog of some 600,000 houses, and for the first time required local authorities to submit plans. Early generosity in subsidies was soon curtailed and successive administrations variously cut and expanded the programmes. By the time, in the 1930s, that local authorities were rerouted into slum clearance, they and private builders had produced some 2,200,000 houses and largely wiped out the deficit in the effective demand for houses. Even on low standards of accommodation, however, there was still in 1939 a shortage of some half a million houses, to complete slum clearance and reduce overcrowding. Furthermore, local authorities never really managed to keep the rents down sufficiently for the poorest families, so that many of these remained in very bad conditions in private rented accommodation.[26]

A loss of some 450,000 houses in World War II, not to mention serious dilapidation and virtually no new building, left the 1945 Labour Government in considerable difficulty, which was soon enhanced by a rising family formation rate. They also started with high standards and generous subsidies (after a crash programme of prefab building), but austerity and inflation again soon whittled this away. Local authorities again were the main builders, and at first little private building was allowed. By 1952, however, private building was in full swing, and in 1955–56 local authorities were once more put on to slum clearance. It is of note that their responsibility to provide homes only for the working classes was generalised in 1949. Nevertheless, whether under general building or slum clearance, local authorities remain primarily concerned to provide housing mainly for working-class people.

A national survey carried out in 1964[27] found that 77 per cent of heads of households in council housing were manual workers; but also that there were 69 per cent in unfurnished private housing with controlled rents; and 60 per cent in private housing where the rents were not controlled. The highest proportion in the Registrar General's social Classes IV and V are found in the controlled sector (39 per cent as against 36 per cent in local authorities and 27 per cent in private uncontrolled housing). Those people in controlled, and to a lesser extent in uncontrolled, private unfurnished accommodation are mainly old people, and the controlled have the highest proportion (40 per cent—much higher than any other sector—of those with heads of households having an income of less than £7 10s. p.w.).

This illustrates the point that the major problems of providing working-class housing are still by no means solved. There is considerable difficulty in providing accommodation suitable in size, quality and location, at low enough rents, in a situation where the actual cost of land and construction is much too high to do so on an economic basis; and in making sure that the people who need it most get it. Although there has recently been considerable government encouragement of housing societies and associations, the financial conditions under which they work do not make it possible for them to let at rents low enough for most working-class families; the responsibility remains firmly with the local authorities.

Owner occupation is, however, steadily advancing (occupying about 3 per cent p.a. more dwellings in the period 1960–64), and it is worth noting that in 1964, 47 per cent of all owner occupiers were manual workers, although a substantial proportion of these must have been owners of the poorer type of property. It is not clear how far manual workers would buy their own houses if they could. Both the Rowntree surveys[28] and the 1964 survey show that those who wish to rent are older, more often manual workers, and have lower incomes than those who wish to buy; but older people are less likely to get mortgages (a half of those wanting to rent in 1964 were over fifty), and are also more likely to be cautious in taking on extra responsibilities. It may well be that the younger generation of manual workers will more often buy houses, especially as recent changes give better terms for intending buyers paying lower rates of income tax. The recent poverty study[8] showed that a higher proportion of the younger parents were owner occupiers. There is also a move towards the sale of houses by local authorities (about 5,000 were sold in 1966 out of a stock of about 5 million, of these 1,000 having been built for sale; this represents a considerable increase over any previous year, particularly in the sale of houses built before 1939).[29]

Nevertheless, the majority of working-class people are likely for some time to come to live either in the older privately owned houses or in council housing. Due to slum clearance, the majority of the lower paid workers are likely to move into council housing, which already has a large majority of manual workers. Much of this is of the standard three-bedroom type and it is only in recent years that the numbers of dwellings suitable for old people or large families have been increasing, so that council housing tends to be somewhat overcrowded. There is also a good deal of it which is no longer up to modern standards; and in addition it must not be forgotten that the large urban authorities own considerable amounts of old property, much of it, but not all, likely to be demolished in the not too distant future. In 1964, 7 per cent of all those renting from local authorities were in houses built before 1919.

It is not clear what happens to low income families, since authorities vary enormously in whether or not they run rent rebate or similar schemes, and on the benefits given under them; and the increased cost of the journey to work is often a deterrent. A proportion of these families may well move into equally unsuitable low rent housing instead of accepting rehousing from the local authority; it is to be hoped this is not a high proportion. So far as deviant low income families (problem families) are concerned, authorities often deliberately move these into sub-standard accommodation instead of new housing. There is also an unanswered question as to what proportion of low income families move back into poorer but cheaper accommodation either because they find the costs too high, or because the neighbours tend to be critical of them, or both.

In general, it would appear from the poverty study that those with the lowest incomes and largest families are more often in local authority accommodation. Of those below the national assistance levels in 1966, 54 per cent were in local authority accommodation as against 32 per cent of those above these levels; 17 per cent were owner-occupiers and 18 per cent rented other types of accommodation, the rest being non-householders or not known. What type of local authority accommodation they occupied is not clear, but presumably the 23 per cent lacking basic amenities were those in private housing. The largest families are more often overcrowded and more often live in defective housing when they have very low incomes.

Being a council tenant tends to reduce geographical mobility, as it is very difficult to get on to a housing list elsewhere because of locality rules. It is likely that the trend towards owner occupation in the younger generation, and the requirements of the economy, will gradually force fundamental changes in the allocation policy of local authorities for dwellings other than those immediately necessary for rehousing slum clearance families.

The working class has always had the worst housing, and this situation is only slowly easing. The decline of the private rented sector which contains most of the older, poorer quality housing is obviously of considerable benefit providing suitable alternatives are available; the lack of these and the amount of conversion into high rent property has led to a considerable problem of homelessness in London which still persists. Outside London the effects have not been quite so startling, but the slow demolition of houses found unfit on the extremely low standards of the 1957 Housing Act definition, means that many of these will continue to be lived in for a considerable period to come. Local authorities in England and Wales reported 771,000 houses unfit at the beginning of 1965 and twenty-four local authorites are responsible for dealing with half of these.[30] In 1966 the annual number of unfit dwellings cleared had crept up to 65,000, having been about 61,000–62,000 in the previous five years, but the twenty-four authorities concerned have been clearing them at only about a third of that rate. Perhaps there will be a considerable speed-up in the provision of new housing, which is the major bottleneck, but since this largely depends upon acquiring overspill sites and starting new towns, it seems a little unlikely. If we remember that the figures quoted probably represent only the worst of the unfit and that there are many more which are not far off this standard, the immediate prospect for the considerable areas in the North and in Scotland, which are the ones mainly concerned, is not bright.

Donnison[31] calculates that at a building rate of 485,000 new units per annum in Great Britain (i.e. excluding Northern Ireland), about 160,000 would be needed for increases in the number of households; 20,000 to reduce sharing; 30,000 for increasing vacancies in order to provide for mobility, 30,000 to replace demolitions other than for slum clearance (e.g. for roads), and conversions to other uses. This would leave somewhere about 240–250,000 for replacing obsolete housing. This is based on thirty-year projections reduced to an annual rate. If he means this last figure to be related to clearance rates, as I assume he does, we have a long way to go to achieve this, since clearance in Great Britain is running only at some 75,000 dwellings a year.

If, in addition, we wish to provide even the basic amenities for those houses not cleared, we shall have to move fast on this front also. In 1961 22 per cent of households in England and Wales had no bath. Even if the numbers of families rehoused from clearance rose to a rate of 220,000 in 1970 and remained there subsequently, it would take until 1981 to provide all these people with baths. If installation of baths under improvement grants were to go on at the present rate this would bring the date forward three or four years. A much more rapid rate of improvement must obviously accompany clearance, if the basic amenities are to be provided in the near future.

The traditional working class

We have now dealt with a number of major spheres affecting life and living and indicated how they affect the working class; but important as they are, discussing these sectors does not convey any real understanding of the quality of working-class life. Unfortunately, it is a matter for discussion and some dispute exactly what has happened in recent years. Considerable inroads have obviously been made into ways of living and thinking which were slow to change, but the long tradition of working-class life remains strong. In this chapter, therefore, we outline briefly what is usually described as 'the traditional working class', remembering, however, that while many of the points made remain important, what is being described is a stereotype which may no longer exist as a whole, though its parts, in changed forms, still remain very strong in a number of parts of the country.

The traditional working-class community has something of the nature of a string of overlapping urban villages, life being contained within the narrow area within which poverty and low social and geographical mobility confined the extended family. Furthermore, the limited range and importance of education, maintained until recently a largely oral transmission of custom and ritual directly descended from the original villages, some four or five generations back. Seabrook, whose family moved into the town only three generations ago (in the 1860s) records that some of the older members of his family could still recite fragments of the Christmas Mummers play, and remember May Day songs and the Plough Monday procession.

In the industrial society many of the limitations of the village remained. The forces which affected their jobs were as incomprehensible and uncontrollable as those which led to crop failure; trade unions could only provide a limited degree of protection from arbitrary action and poverty. Movement was extremely limited, largely because of poverty; and it was normal to live in the same area, surrounded by one's family for the whole of one's life. Education increasingly became a way out for a minority—a great-aunt of Seabrook's became a schoolteacher at the instigation of the family she went to as a domestic at the age of twelve, who paid for her education. This must have been around 1900. A more common fate was suffered by one of his aunts who passed an examination at thirteen, which entitled her to be transferred to the high school, but her mother badly needed her earnings and she went into the boot factory instead. Classroom education was clearly not of much use in a community which was poverty stricken and, with reason, saw only a future of manual work for the boys and marriage for the girls. Most members of the working class agreed with many of their 'betters' that a minimum of reading, writing and arithmetic was all the working man or woman needed.

To poverty, immobility and limited education add the age-old subjection of women, and the stage is set for the major elements of traditional working-class life. Life on the edge of unemployment, sickness, starvation, and death, bore hardest on the women who drew heavily upon their families, and particularly their mothers, for help and comfort. Marriage and motherhood were almost their only access to prestige—as indeed they had been for generations—and the position of 'Mum' was very much enhanced as a result. The men had less need of kin to support them, since they were able to exercise what autonomy was possible within the limitations of their circumstances, and remained attached to friends, the local, and a limited degree of gambling. (In a small community news travels fast, and male friends were not only more congenial, but also safer.)

For the most part, they probably indulged in all these things in moderation. It is easy to overemphasise the degree of drinking, gambling and neglect of wives and families, since contemporary accounts tend to fasten upon the more dramatic and the highly reprehensible. Traditionally, the men were inclined to go their own way, but remained ready to do men's work in the home and to fulfil their responsibilities to their families in those ways which were open to them. The regulars at the pubs at times other than weekends were more often the detached, the isolated and the unmarried; the settled married man could not afford it and he read the paper or did jobs about the house.

An emphasis on manual work, and limited education, led to difficulties in communication both in speech and writing; this further accentuated the separation of roles and the problems of dealing with children, and reduced the possibility of mobility and contact with a wide range of people, especially those who spoke fluently with a 'posh' accent and were in positions of authority. Experience told the working man and woman that no one but themselves was going to help them to deal with their problems; and authority was likely to be harmful—the poor law official and the evangelist were equally alien. Poor ability in communication also made it more difficult to deal with people unless one had known them a long time, that is kin and friendship groups. In any case kinship relationships were extensive and local and heavily strengthened by prevailing values.

That the communication difficulty is still strong is instanced by the work of Bernstein, who has commented on the 'restricted' speech of the working class and the fact that it tends to clothe a largely non-conceptual mode of thought. There is no very concrete evidence, however, concerning how far this is so in what section of the working class, and it is doubtful if it would apply as much to the upper, as to the middle and lower strata. Nor is it clear whether the young are better or worse in this respect than the older people. Characters like the father in David Storey's *Flight to Camden*, full of bottled emotion and only capable of expressing it in action, are common in fiction, but is the greater fluency of the young fact or fiction?

The maintenance of the kinship system became, and to a considerable extent remains, a value in itself. (The Swansea study records an incident in which a nephew whose family they had not seen since they moved to Lancashire years ago, knocked on the door unexpectedly, and was immediately welcomed and lodged for four months. It would have been unthinkable to do otherwise.) Similarly the overriding value of kinship in itself was expressed in acceptance with as much tolerance as one could muster of unlikeable people in the family, and of attendance at family functions; weddings and funerals in particular. The importance of being good to Mum remains deeply ingrained, even to the extent of boys at a probation camp, after having spent their money, stealing a present to take home to her.

The need for endurance, the requirements of manual work, and the close proximity in which most people lived with the minority of the population who were given to violence led to a great emphasis on physical toughness, one manifestation of which is reluctance to admit illness. It was necessary not to be deterred by bad weather, cold water, or restricted diet, and this led to a strong feeling against 'pampering' either of children or adults. Much self-expression in the men took the form of exhibitions of toughness; in young men this could lead to a good deal of fighting.

Along with physical toughness went a necessary toughness of mind. Stubbornness has been a trait often admired in the working class, partly as a substitute for thought where this is at a discount. There was a distinct strain of anti-intellectualism, only partly abated by the acceptance of study for a concrete purpose such as part of an apprenticeship. Activity was important, and reading was equivalent to not doing anything at all, only acceptable if it was for one's entertainment. This did not, and does not, prevent the women possessing a vast store of knowledge about family and domestic matters; or the men, especially more recently, performing considerable feats of memory in connection with sporting events, and showing quite considerable prowess in betting arithmetic. Nevertheless, the working class probably more than other sectors of the population has decried book-learning. Argument is usually by assertion and counter assertion ('it stands to reason'), under which supporting structures of selected 'facts' are built. Wisdom and good sense, that is, a practical way out of a concrete situation, are much prized, and informal leaders tended to have this, as well as considerable stubbornness and pugnacity.

5

The steady and repetitive nature of everyday living for both men and women, and lack of expectation of change, has put a premium on things which are exciting. In adolescence this comes out as actually experiencing thrills, but for the older person it is very much in terms of gambling. Gambling has always been popular throughout the class structure, though probably least emphasised in the lower middle class. It was of special importance to the working class since it not only introduced an element of excitement and expectation, but also the possibility of an unexpected windfall which could be spent on entertainment or necessities.

The pressure of continuous hardship at work and at home gave rise also to the occasional junkets: the more regular weekend drinking and later, cinema-going; the firm outing; the Christmas bank holidays. Some of these were heavily reinforced by their emphasis on kinship solidarity: christenings, marriages, funerals. There were lesser things, too, as Hoggart records: the bit of ham for tea, fish and chip suppers, the cheap ornaments and toys, sets of darts, pigeons, extra articles of clothing, and, later, wireless and television, paid for with money which might well have been spent on food, but which provided the necessary sources of pleasure in things to ensure self-respect, to give status, to enjoy leisure.

What has been described as a high density of relationships has advantages in the form of support, but also disadvantages in terms of intrusion on privacy. There thus grew up, on the one hand, a feeling of community support and on the other a strong tendency towards autonomy and independence. Keeping yourself to yourself has always been of great importance, since the revelation of trials, emotions or quarrels, is not only dangerous in a closely knit community where news spreads fast, but is a threat to the confidence of others who are also proudly independent. Within the family one may be able to talk—and even then often only with selected confidants. But living in other people's pockets implies at least an outward conformity, and this also furthers the use of commonly accepted ideas and attitudes of a necessarily superficial nature, from which departure is likely to cause unease.

Thus, as the various studies agree, 'neighbouring' turns out to be a rather superficial relationship. People do help each other, house-wives gossip, men borrow tools; but the persistent borrower is a pest, is disliked, and identifies herself as a bad manager, and the general recognition of acquaintances and neighbours is supportive of feelings of community, but not of primary importance.

Autonomy is, however, independence within a set of known relationships and towards outsiders it can become rejecting. 'We keep ourselves to ourselves' is a fundamentally exclusive sentiment. The rejections have applied as much to middle-class people as to the Irish, the Poles and anyone else with an accent, and more recently to coloured immigrants. They are all intruders to be re-garded with suspicion. Immigrants are more immediately an intru-sion and tend to be regarded as lazy, dirty, smelly and promiscuous. If they also keep themselves to themselves and turn out to be hard-working, clean and firmly married—that is, if they demonstrate what are not only working-class virtues, but general virtues—they are likely to be accepted in time, although obviously competitition for housing or work may defer acceptance. It is difficult to prove them-selves, because those who lapse confirm the original suspicions. It is a hard upward climb, from 'all of you' through 'not you, of course' to 'they're all people like us'.

Hoggart devotes a good deal of space to 'Them' but he makes it clear at the outset that 'not you, of course' applies very strongly. 'Them' is a generic term for all those people who control your destinies, in industry, in politics, in the government. Working-class people are often at a considerable disadvantage. Their lives tend to be public in many ways; if they get drunk it is more likely to be in the pub, and if as a result there is a friendly but violent argument, they are liable to get arrested. If they go to the doctor, or the hospital, or the labour exchange, or the social security office, or to the town hall, they are likely to be kept waiting for long periods. They often come in contact with the people on the counter who are the lower grades of minor official and may well be rude or rushed, or officious. What is more, these people administer a mass of complex regulations which it is virtually impossible to understand, but which only too often seem to work against the applicant.

From time to time, those in high places change things for reasons which are usually quite incomprehensible. In the past the working class has been torn between a belief that everybody is doing his best and the situation really is impossible—Baldwin was a past master at conveying this impression, while failing signally to have any grasp of world or home affairs—and an equally strong belief that they are being 'done'. The creation of the National Health Service did a tremendous amount for working-class confidence, and, despite what the experts say about its deficiencies, the P.E.P. survey[1] shows that it is very strongly approved. The N.H.S. has also benefited from the rapid advance of medical technology. More and more you can not only get 'something that does you good' but it really does you good. And you've paid for it, and you're entitled to it. On the other hand, unless you are a strong Labour supporter, it is difficult to avoid the belief that pensions could easily be put up if only 'They' cut something else.

Attitudes to 'Them' have probably softened as a result of the welfare state and release for most from dire poverty. But it remains true that 'there isn't much you can do about it whatever happens'; and the reaction, as Hoggart further suggests, is withdrawal rather than participation. After a hundred years of poverty, the working class might well be excused for sitting back and enjoying twenty years of comparative ease.

Another aspect of the feeling of solidarity which both gives rise to and is supported by the rejection of 'Them', has been a strong feeling that working-class people ought not to 'give themselves airs' and put themselves above their fellows, and there is thus a reluctance to occupy leadership positions. This remains very strong among the women who are very quick to criticise any attempt to organise them; although they will accept membership of church groups, where the minister or his wife forms a readymade organiser. Amongst the men, the long tradition of trade unionism has broken this down much more, but there is still a reluctance to take up clear leadership roles, and both trade union local leaders and those in supervisory grades in industry have to be careful to avoid an authoritarian approach. Leadership both promotes solidarity and is a threat to it, and in this dilemma the tendency is to choose solidarity based on informal rather than formal relationships.

The problems of maintaining life, individuality and self-respect given the conditions under which the working class have traditionally lived, may well have been solved in many ways. Given the cultural traditions of Western European and particularly British society, they were bound to involve emphasis on the nuclear and extended family, upon the limitation of the overt expression of sexuality, upon justice and fairness and upon regular work as a source of income and as a form of prestige.

Since every social sanction involves the possibility of failing to abide by it, proximity, crowding, the emphasis on physical strength and virility in men, and of subjection in women, and the need for excitement, led also to disruptive influences. Most feared by the women in their men were drunkenness, gambling and sexual adventures; the dangers for the men lay mainly in violence, in the shrewishness of dissatisfied women and their failures as housekeepers and mothers; and in the varieties of injustice and humiliation which could derive from their weak position at work, and insecurity in their jobs.

Above all, the working class remained close to the failures of their culture—the people who, through illness or deficiencies, mental or physical, weakness of character or sheer pressure of hardship, had gone under, and given up the fight against dirt, poverty, unemployment, the needs of children, and the ever present temptations of drink, sex, theft, or deliberately living on charity. For the working class as for other classes, these were the undeserving poor, the more to be condemned; though more clearly perceived and understood because they themselves avoided the abyss only through constant effort and self-restraint. To keep one's self-respect was more than a traditional value, it was a condition of survival.

The personal; the concrete; the immediate solution of the problem; the commitment of the whole self to enjoyments when they come; crowded living and the comfort of being with those you know and understand in familiar places, pride in providing for and managing home and family and in not being beholden to others—these give rise to the strengths and weaknesses of traditional working-class life. Those who have been part of it, and are able to describe it, find it difficult not to show their dislike for it (D. H. Lawrence, Seabrook), or their admiration (Walter Greenwood, Hoggart). The studies listed in chapter 1 contain a number of descriptions by informed and skilled observers. Yet the uncertainty in the use of the past or present tense in what has been said above, only reflects a real uncertainty as to how much of it remains relevant. It is generally thought that the lower the stratum, the further north the area, and the more isolated the industrial community, the more likelihood there is of the persistence of the basic characteristics. But we do not really know if traditional working-class life as described above continues to exist anywhere without important changes, varying in type and degree from one place to another. Most of this book therefore, must be taken equally as a commentary upon possible trends and as an analysis of what is actually happening.

The life cycle

6

In his original study of poverty, Rowntree comments upon the different stages in the life of the working-class family. He called this the 'poverty cycle' since severe poverty was almost inevitable at some period. Poverty is now less inevitable but the stages are still important. It is not that they are essentially different in any other part of the population, but that the nature of working-class life gives them a particular quality of their own.

Traditionally childhood is a time of considerable freedom in which the street group plays an increasingly important part. The boys are freer than the girls, who tend to have younger siblings put into their care fairly early on. In adolescence friendship groups became particularly important, and are strengthened by the long period those concerned have already known each other. Adolescence has traditionally been a brief period of flowering before adult responsibilities take over. This is particularly so for the girls, now temporarily released from small children, conscious that they will marry early, and as time goes on, increasingly aware that they will lose status if they do not (the sad extreme of this short summer is dramatised in Sheila Delaney's *A Taste of Honey*).

Marriage temporarily cuts the young man from his mates and the girl from her kin, but the patterns re-establish themselves as children appear. By the time he is married the man is well on the way to attaining his maximum pay and has settled into working, but there is more job changing, and a greater possibility of variation in pay packets than is usually assumed. The wife continues to earn and they are reasonably well off, although burdened with hire purchase commitments.

When the first baby comes, the wife leaves work and income is radically reduced, but this may be offset by increased overtime earnings, or moving to a higher paid job. (The Labour Mobility Survey shows that married men more often work longer hours than single, although the proportion working over forty-eight hours per week is lower in the unskilled.) The wife tends to stay off work during most of the period when the children are small unless there are special reasons (among which low earnings of the husband, or high aspirations for material possessions are both important). Where there are large families closely spaced, as in the lower stratum, there is increasing hardship, especially as it is less likely that the wife will go back to work for a long period, or at all. The husband tends to drift back to his friends and the local, but his activities are also circumscribed by shortage of funds. More often nowadays he continues to take some positive part in dealing with the children, and he decorates or gardens or pursues some hobby. As the children grow they become more expensive and the strain increases. This may lead to a stronger separation of roles, but it may lead to more mutual support. The fact that the husband spends some time at the pub or club is accepted and acceptable providing he also fulfils his role as husband and father.

The financial strain is gradually relieved when the children begin to earn. A large family then becomes an advantage because there may be several earners on adult rates of pay. They gradually marry and leave, and the parents are left on their own, but usually with the family living fairly near, and in and out. There is then a period of comparative comfort and tranquillity (providing they get on with each other), which is ended by a shrinkage of income on retirement. In the normal case the family continues to see that the parents are all right and to provide a good deal in kind, though tactfully avoiding giving cash (which they may be short of themselves at this period). If the mother dies first the father is taken care of usually by one of the daughters. The real casualties of old age, and those who are likely to be in hospitals or homes, are those without family, or with no family nearby, or who have fallen out with their families (quite possibly their own fault).

Postwar changes in marriage rates, fertility rates, combined with the strong trend mentioned earlier towards increasing proportions of women in the thirty-five to fifty age group to be at work, are already leading to important changes in the cycle. For the last thirty years there has been a trend towards women marrying earlier, and there has been an increase in the proportion of women married. The younger they marry, the more children they have; and this, combined with an increasing birth rate has led to projections of rather higher family sizes than previously: the mean ultimate family size for women marrying in 1940 who had thus completed their families was as low as two, but this was presumably affected by wartime conditions. After a steady increase from 1955 to 1964, the number of births has shown a slight decline, and the most recent projections available at the time of writing,[1] show a mean ultimate family size for those married in 1955 as 3·10 for women under twenty at marriage, 2·33 for those between twenty and twenty-four and 2·00 for those between twenty-five and twenty-nine: for all those under forty-five, 2·34. The corresponding projections for those married in 1964 are 3·11, 2·14, 2·06 and 2·51, while the much more problematical figures for those marrying in 1984 are 3·22, 2·45, 2·11 and 2·67. It is impossible to say whether the changes in recent years have anything to do with greatly increased efficiency of contraception, and what long term effect this will have.

Since the trend towards earlier marriage is more pronounced in the working class, and family size increases as one goes down the scale (but will it continue to do so, or will the differences at least be reduced?), the mean ultimate family size is likely to be on the high rather than the low side. However, the increasing size of the skilled manual group tends to affect the figures very much and they are much more akin to the middle class—indeed the foreman and supervisors' group seems to be very near the intermediate and senior non-manual grades who have consistently shown the lowest figures throughout the century.

In general, however, these changes mean that the working-class wife is likely to get back to work fairly early, probably in her thirties, and there will be two incomes for most of the period of the marriage. She will still be in her forties when the family is working and earning, still working and of limited support to her daughters who have small children, but she will leave work if they really need help. Greater mobility will be offset by higher car ownership (the Swansea study comments upon the continuance of family visiting by car), and while the mothers and daughters will not live quite so much in each other's pockets, they will eventually resume patterns of frequent visiting as the daughters get used to the idea of driving a car—still not very usual in the working class where cars fall in the male sphere of activity (it is doubtful incidentally, if most projections of car usage take this factor into account sufficiently). Presumably the installation and use of telephones will also spread far down into the working class.

It is to be hoped that the income drop on retirement will not be quite so serious by the end of the century. However, even assuming that the birth rate does not rise to unprecedented heights, the dependency ratio (children plus old people as a proportion of the working population) will increase steadily, since a falling off towards the end of the period in the proportion (not numbers) of old people, will be more than counterbalanced by a considerable increase in the proportion of children. The pressure upon available resources will, therefore, continue. It is unlikely that the divorce and separation rates will rise so steeply as to offset the effects of the higher marriage rate in producing families for old people to lean on. Even though the breakdown rate for early marriages is higher, we do not know what the trend will be in remarriage. We also do not know what proportion of unsupported women with illegitimate children will remain unsupported. Those with one child are liable to have a second chance for marriage when the child grows up, especially as there is a slight shortage of women as against men.

We deal separately with young people and the old, and the rest of this chapter is concerned with the other stages in the cycle.

Courtship

It is probably the pattern throughout the social classes that after a period of going out with different people in an experimental way, couples eventually settle down to a fairly regular dating. Schofield[2] shows that, so far as sexual intercourse goes, the boys are more active with more partners; but that a smaller number of girls are involved, and that they are likely to be dating steadily. It is, of course, a common pattern in our society that the girl's acceptance of intercourse is an indication that she wants a permanent relationship with the boy.

In the working class the stronger tradition of close and continuing male friendship groups sets a problem for the girls who have to detach the boys from their friends while at the same time not allowing too serious a form of sex play. The mixture of sexuality and drift on the boy's part, and of respectability and choice on the girl's, is superbly described in Stan Barstow's novel *A Kind of Loving*. Equally well described is the strength of the structure of 'doing what's right'. When Ingrid becomes pregnant, Vic accepts almost without question that he must marry her; the mothers are defensive, the fathers concerned but sensible, they are all torn between 'doing what's right' and doing what's best for Ingrid and Vic, and 'doing what's right' wins out, very much on the assumption that this is the way marriages tend to occur anyway, you have to learn to live as best you can in the married state, and more often than not it all turns out reasonably well.

In the lower working class, and particularly amongst the deviants, the pattern is somewhat distorted for several reasons. The very much reduced degree of interpersonal understanding leads more often to demands for intercourse by the boys which the girls cannot deny, and indeed would not feel it right to deny, and thus very much increases the risk of illegitimacy, As in many other things, marriage is entered into more lightly, and with more serious consequences.

Marriage

It has already been pointed out that low mobility leads to a situation where there are considerable numbers of extended and intermarried families living within a comparatively short compass. The Crown

Street sample, which was considerably larger than that taken in the Bethnal Green study where this point was much emphasised, showed that 70 per cent of heads of households, and 76 per cent of wives born in the areas had parents who had lived or were living in the areas; 33 per cent of husbands and 53 per cent of wives had parents still living nearby, and 40 per cent had brothers or sisters. A similar result was found in Swansea also with a large sample, although with a wider geographical scatter, offset by a high car ownership. All studies of the areas less affected by rehousing or other changes agree on this point.

A similar agreement is found about the role of the wife's mother. The mother–daughter relationship is bound to be cemented to a considerable extent by similar interests in any social class, but it is of much greater importance where they are both coping with low incomes and large families. Even without this, during the period when there are small children, the need for baby sitting, for consultation, support and advice is great and much more easily satisfied if 'Mum' is near at hand, and Mum may well be a more important influence than is the health visitor, as the Nottingham study demonstrates. The dependence on Mum can, in fact, lead to extremes, where the wife tends to see little of her former friends. 'Since we've had the children, I've got no more friends—outside the family, I mean,' said one married woman in Bethnal Green, and another: 'I don't see my best friend much. She's married too, and she's always round her Mum's, like I'm always round mine.'

The Swansea study gives figures comparing frequency of contact in the middle and working classes (carefully distinguished on claimed class as well as occupation), which throw some light upon the mother–daughter relationship. The significant differences are in the daily contacts and do not show up in the weekly contacts, and they thus seem to relate to proximity. Rosser and Harris continue the tradition of emphasising the importance of the relationship, but it is not clear if it differs in quality when physical separation intervenes, and it seems very doubtful whether it then differs at all from a substantial section of the middle class.

It is very common for the newly-weds to agree to live either with or near the wife's family. In Crown Street, 28 per cent of the families originally lived with the wife's parents as against 12 per cent with the husband's parents. The same trend is clearly observable in relation to parents living within a quarter of a mile; and elsewhere in Liverpool. It would appear, however, that there is a substantial minority where the wives do not live near their parents or live with the husband's parents, so that this point must not be overemphasised.

It is, however, obviously more likely that the wife will get on better with her mother in sharing a kitchen (if she must, because of housing shortage, share with someone), and she will obtain more support from her if living nearby. 'A son's your son till he gets a wife, but a daughter's your daughter for all your life', a tag quoted both in the Bethnal Green and Crown Street studies, is far more generally true than of the working class alone, but is much more relevant where there is a long term need and therefore a stronger reliance on the family's duty to help.

Mum-centredness is particularly a function of that period of the life cycle where her children have grown up and married, leaving Mum, if she is still young enough, and hale enough after the strains of bringing up her family, as an active and useful centre of family life, extremely influential because of her experience, and strongly motivated to keep her children round her. Where separation of conjugal roles has left her little in common with her husband, this tendency is enhanced. As one Bethnal Green dustman said, with unconscious poetry 'Mum's is the central depot in this family'. In these circumstances there are regular gatherings on Saturdays and Sundays at Mum's house and these usually include the daughters' husbands and children.

It is, however, a point to be noted that the pervasive mother-in-law joke is strongly biased towards the wife's mother. Both the repetition of the subject and the need to treat it humorously indicate a situation of strain in the relationship. There is not much evidence in the studies of the husband's feelings about the system; but it would appear that, on the one hand he sees the good sense—and the convenience for himself—of exchange of services between the wife and her kin; and on the other, he is less likely to be heavily involved in these relationships anyway as he can more easily escape into work and leisure. Both D. H. Lawrence and Hoggart have described with eloquence the strong feeling of sons for their mothers, and this persists in terms of visiting and general support, but it is weakened by lack of role similarity.

It must be noted that the studies do not provide much real information about the way in which the mother–son relationship fits into the picture. It is clear that the men do not see their parents as often as the wives do, but no attempt has been made to link this with the much greater restriction of time they have available in which to do so. The Bethnal Green general sample shows that of the men, 30 per cent saw their fathers and 31 per cent their mothers in the previous twenty-four hours, as against 48 per cent and 55 per cent for the women. If one reckons that half the day or more (including overtime) is spent by the men at work or travelling, this would appear to be a strikingly high proportion, and no evidence of lack of contact at all. There also seems to be little information about who is consulted in relation to important family decisions. Perhaps under-emphasis of the male point of view is associated with the greater availability and readiness to talk of the women. In some of the studies, notably Ship Street and Branch Street, there seems to have been very little contact between the research worker and the men.

Constant contact between wife and mother tends to exacerbate the tendency towards separation of conjugal roles. The Ashton study brings out very clearly the continuance of the adolescent peer group friendships into adulthood, only marginally affected by marriage; but this is a rather special situation in a somewhat isolated and small community dominated by one industry where there is a considerable degree of fusion of work and non-work roles. The pattern is either less noticeable or less commented upon in Radby. There is no comment upon the fact that, if it is true that there is a considerable degree of matrilocality in family living, it is more likely that the husband will have his friendship groups disrupted by movement than the wife. In the older generations, attachment to a limited neighbourhood may be strongly felt, since there has been less experience of easy travelling. Differences in adjoining streets which it is difficult for the outside observer to appreciate, bulk large in the thinking of both men and women, so that what appears to be a quite short move may lead to a considerable change in terms of friendship groups.

Separation of conjugal roles is due to a number of reasons. Bott,[3] whose capacity for insightful speculation far outruns the impact of data collected from twenty families, lays much emphasis on the supposition that where both husband and wife come from closeknit networks of relatives, family allegiance tends to pull them apart, but this does not square with the unequal strength of kin allegiance in husband and wife. As the Swansea study points out, where much of family living is shared (what Bott calls a 'joint' as against a 'segregated' marital relationship), it is still possible to have many friends in common, even if kinship networks are separated.

The status and attitudes of the woman in the marriage are, of course, important. There is a much stronger likelihood that the working-class woman will be heavily domesticated and accept the position that the man is 'the meister' but there are also a variety of other things. As Zweig points out, commenting on the change from poverty to affluence, poverty meant that money for leisure outings is limited, but it also went with extremely adverse working conditions, much insecurity in holding one's job, work pressure and anxiety. In addition what Klein describes as 'cognitive poverty'—considerable difficulty in expressing oneself in words, and of attaining a real understanding of other people—made communication difficult. Poverty leads to arguments about money, and in a situation of cognitive poverty, these are more likely to lead to rows than discussions. Above all, the weight of the sanctions surrounding the institution of monogamous marriage in western society, despite considerable changes, still leaves the husband in a position which it is easy for him to exploit if he so wishes. The weapons open to the wife are largely in terms of the handling of a difficult relationship and require a high level of social skill, especially where strains are high. The elevation of endurance, and the actual bearing and bringing up of children, into a status system amongst the women (well described by Hoggart and Seabrook) is a consequence of their weak bargaining position.

Nevertheless, the picture of the traditional working-class family as being one where the husband is never home, and when he is he may well be drunk or violent, is a considerable distortion. In Walter Greenwood's *Love on the Dole* it is the 'villains' who are always in the pub, not the heroes. Indeed, the extra burden of loss of wife's earnings and of the children themselves, more often than not led, and still lead, to considerable restriction in the husband's ability to drink or gamble. Even in Ashton men were often home, and the persistence of separation of roles was then in terms of allotments or do-it-yourself at home, that is, of men's and women's work. This remains a by no means uncommon pattern in all strata below the point where many of these jobs are carried out by others and paid for.

A number of the studies of the working class cite as evidence of the separation of roles lack of knowledge amongst wives of the nature of their husband's job, and of his earnings. It is very doubtful if most middle-class wives could say exactly what their husbands do, or how much they earn. What is probably different is a stronger acceptance of the woman's 'wage' and of the man's right to dispose of the surplus without consultation; and the consequences of the normal tendency of the male to exploit his autonomy in a situation where they are, for the wife, much more serious. The degree of exploitation probably increases as one moves down the working-class strata, but it is clear from the Radby study that it is for the most part considered to have boundaries which bring down male as well as female disapproval on those who exceed them. After all, both male authority and male benevolence in marriage are traditional Christian values.

It is not easy to say with any clarity, therefore, to what degree separation of conjugal roles existed or exists in the traditional working class. What seems likely is that the strains of poverty, insecurity and overcrowding, the emphasis upon the importance of physical strength as against 'learning', the poor quality of the educational system and its failure to appreciate the value of the spoken word, and the advantages and disadvantages of living in a closely interwoven network of kin, all contributed to a considerable slowing down of the trend towards the personalising of women. The pattern of husband–wife relationships in the traditional working class remains more faithful to the historically normal situation, amongst the majority of the population in all countries, of male authority; and to the age-old belief, held by both sexes, that women are lesser beings, subordinate to men. It should not be forgotten also that the separation of roles has the advantage of providing comparatively simple and well understood spheres of activities; and of standards for attaining self-respect by successfully fulfilling the roles. Negotiation between equals is exceedingly difficult to handle in the complex emotion-laden atmosphere of the marital relationship, and the younger generation may well ponder the possibility of frying pans and fires.

The release from poverty for most of the working class, coupled in many cases with a general loosening of the kinship network, has allowed the trend towards the personalising of women to follow more closely the middle-class trend; and, while separation of roles in its older forms continues in the older people, the newer form in which more decisions are taken jointly, there is more discussion, and a smaller proportion of the men are heavily involved in male friendship groups associated with pubs and clubs, is more prevalent in the younger generation. An unexplored key area is those parts of the younger generation who are still subject to many of the pressures outlined above. Most of the material about joint marital relationships seems to refer either to situations where the couples have moved from choice on to new estates or are experiencing the shock of a forced removal through slum clearance, or to the distinctly affluent worker such as Zweig's group, or the sample being studied by Goldthorpe and Lockwood.[4] It is probably true that income alone is not the major factor, since there is a great deal of overlapping between income ranges in the lower strata of the working class. It is not clear what does govern changes in marital role relationships; or indeed to what degree they have changed and in which strata.

Other relatives

The studies are so obsessed with the mother–daughter relationship that very little is said about other relatives. Sisters are in closer contact than brothers and presumably, since most of the family contacts are through the wife's mother, the husband sees more of her brothers and sisters than he does of his own, and the children see more of their maternal than their paternal uncles and aunts. Presumably the importance of these relationships depend much more on personal characteristics than kinship ties. Presumably also, the husband has to come to terms with the wife's relations much more than she does with his, and this may produce particular difficulty in coping with his parents in their old age if they need help and have no daughters of their own.

The pressure to marry has always been high in the working class and has if anything become greater recently; but some people stay single. Virtually nothing is known of the problems of these people who stand outside the normal kinship relationships. Hoggart suggests that bachelors are accepted as being harmless deviants, but how far this is generally true is not known.

Sexual problems in marriage

In *A Kind of Loving* Stan Barstow describes the embarrassment of his young hero in buying contraceptives, and his inability to do so contributes to his drift into marriage, much more because the girl wants him than because he wants her. At this stage of life the difficulties are probably general, but exacerbated by the lack of confidence of the working-class boy in an unfamiliar social situation. The inability to cope with the problem of contraception in the traditional working class is again a function of the subjection of women; but is also related to the importance of physical vigour in the men, and the need for an achievement standard for women; most easily translated into terms of unavoidable pregnancies. There are also the straightforward problems of cost; of the lesser effectiveness until recently of female than male contraceptives; and of the inability of the women also to handle a problem involving difficult social skills in approaching doctors and clinics.

There is no real information about English sexual habits other than of adolescents, but Kinsey shows that in the United States there are class differences in sex play. The working class is much less concerned with the preliminaries and with 'heavy petting', and much more inclined to rapid progress to coitus. There has also been a general belief on the part of both sexes that male sexual urges must be fulfilled and that it is both morally and physically bad for the wife, or indeed the girl friend, to deny their fulfilment. In the lower strata where physical strength is more strongly emphasised and the subjection of women is greatest, disagreements tend more often to result in the woman being clobbered; and this includes disagreements over sexual demands. It is more likely also that episodes of rape within marriage will occur; these, however, are probably limited to a very small section.

Pierce and Rowntree[5] reporting on the Population Investigation Committee's Marriage Survey of a sample of 2,338 ever-married informants, show that withdrawal is much more widely used in the working class and particularly in the semiskilled and unskilled categories, than amongst the non-manual grades. However, the patterns of usage amongst skilled workers in cohorts married more than ten years and using contraception from the start of marriage shows little variation from the non-manual patterns. But manual workers are less likely to start contraception at marriage and tend to use it to put the brakes on later on. A comparison of marriage cohorts shows that from those married in the 1930s onwards the proportions using contraceptive methods at some time during marriage vary very little.

It should be remembered that the Catholic population in England is very heavily working-class, and this must affect the figures. The survey found that Catholics more often do not practise contraception, and if they have done so have started later. Those who described themselves as devout less often deviate from the approved method but there was evidence of a general increase in those doing so, particularly after failure in the use of the approved method.

It is probable that the widespread introduction of safe contraceptive methods for women will make a very great difference to the lower stratum. Acceptance of these methods by the Catholic Church would very much enhance this. The pill and the loop are probably of little use in preventing illegitimacy, though they may reduce the proportion of babies born less than nine months after marriage; and they are of doubtful help, because of difficulties in acceptance, in families where there are considerable psychological problems. Nevertheless, they are likely to go a long way towards reducing discord by removing at least one considerable anxiety for the wife, whether or not they actually reduce ultimate family size.

Childbirth and child-rearing

Since the average age of the working-class mother is lower than that of the middle-class mother, and she is also less well informed and more influenced by the traditional lore (sometimes quite horrifying) of her mother and grandmother, the chances are that she will find more difficulty in the antenatal period and in childbirth. The Newsons show from their Nottingham sample that the proportion of mothers, of first and subsequent children, who did relaxation exercises in the working class was half that shown by the middle class. There was also a steady decline from skilled to unskilled manual in the proportion who had first children in hospital, and the middle-class mothers got more than their fair share of places in the maternity hospital, as against wards of general hospitals. Put all these things together and it is likely that the working-class mother though less vocal, suffers much more from the overworked and hardened hospital midwife. She may be left alone in labour, her baby may be taken away for long periods without explanation, and she may be shifted hither and thither and given a stream of medicines and instructions without knowing what is happening or why. A home confinement, even in inconvenient conditions and with an exhausted midwife, at least provides the consolation of familiar surroundings and often enough the presence of a friend or relative (in 43 per cent of all home births, as against none in hospital, according to the Newsons).

In Nottingham it was clear that breast feeding was much more a middle-class than a working-class trait. At one month half of the skilled and semiskilled and 34 per cent of unskilled were still breast feeding as against 60 per cent of the two top classes; and at six months 11 per cent and 7 per cent as against 20 per cent. Middle-class wives have been strongly influenced by the propaganda, but working-class wives are mainly interested in the convenience. They are, however, conscious of the disapproval of health visitors over this and tend to mislead them. The Newsons quote figures from a number of surveys indicating that breast feeding seems to be on the decline.

Another possible explanation for the dislike of breast feeding, despite the extra expense, is that there is often less opportunity for privacy in working-class homes and a much stronger feeling against nakedness, often amounting to prudery, so that a woman may be ashamed of exposing her breast with her husband present.

Working-class babies go on to the bottle earlier and stay on it longer, their mothers being less guilty about the practice. Two- and three-year-olds still partly on the bottle are not uncommon. Similarly 70 per cent of the working-class babies in Nottingham had dummies (the unexpected result here is that over 40 per cent of middle-class mothers also used them—but since then even Dr Spock has become more tolerant about dummies).

The Newsons record a number of other class differences for the under ones. In the working class they go to bed later, they less often sleep in a room alone, their diet is more often inadequate, potty training starts later and is less successful, parents smack their children more, their children more often have temper tantrums, and they much more actively discourage genital play.

In all these things the Newsons confirm the general impression one gets from such studies as Branch Street, Ship Street and Radby that the lower stratum shows the working-class trend in a significantly stronger degree. It is not clear what part of the lower stratum shades off into what we have described as the deviants, and the Radby distinctions are very much a matter of degree and judgment. It is, therefore, virtually impossible to say to what proportion of the working class the following account refers, except that it is probably small.

In these families the baby usually starts off in the same bed as its mother (and father too) and often enough stays there until a new baby arrives, when he is twelve to eighteen months. During this time a great fuss is made of him, but his dispossession is likely to be accompanied by a transfer of attention to the new baby, and from then on he is increasingly on his own. He wanders round the place and in the street sucking his bottle or dummy, and as soon as he is at all safe he is pushed out into the street to fend for himself. He gets little formal training of any kind; in eating, toilet training, speech (since no adult talks to him except to give him orders or to shout at him), or anything else. He will also be subject to the variable temper of the adults in the house who are likely to wallop him or hug him according to how they happen to feel at the moment, and in this they will be reinforcing the uncertainties of life in the street where the older children are also merciless and kindly according to whim. He learns to stick up for himself and grab what he can, and to keep it or give it away when he feels like it. When families of this type are reasonably well off, he is often given money to get rid of him; and he learns that, when this happens, it is important to spend it immediately, and then to consume the proceeds if consumable, or to hide them if not. He also learns the pleasures of being destructive, since the parents have little feeling for preserving property, and in the street might is right.

This type of upbringing tends to produce an unsocialised personality, highly individualistic and egoistic, incapable of curbing his own basic drives, deficient in the skills of handling social relationships in ways which do not involve aggression, unused to and suspicious of affection, and virtually incapable of a solid affectional relationship. That many survive this early training without showing these traits to excess is a tribute to human adaptability. It is usually those where in addition to these problems, serious breakdown and disharmonies in the home or particularly bad handling of the child (often by the father) exists, who come off worse and who constitute a major proportion of the cases dealt with by social work departments and the courts.

For the major part of the working class, however, this account is untrue. Children are treated with a good deal of care by both parents, although in the more traditional working-class oriented areas, the mother takes a much larger responsibility, and the father remains more in the background as a reserve of discipline and authority. A number of studies have been made which throw some light on differences in parental handling in the middle and working classes, but the subject is a difficult one, and the results are somewhat uncertain. Furthermore, they are mainly American and it is not entirely certain they would apply in England. The most comprehensive study of maternal handling of the under-fives[6] shows that middle-class mothers were likely to be less severe in toilet training and to start and end it later; more permissive about eating habits, tidiness or childish evidence of sexual impulses; less likely to hit children or deprive them of privileges; more openly affectionate and less likely to use ridicule as a disciplinary method while using isolation more ('go up to your room'—in the working class the child may not have a room or if he has it may be freezing because it has no easy source of heating).

The differences seem to stem from three sources, already indicated as working-class traits. First there are the difficulties in handling speech and concepts and thus in using persuasion. Secondly, a greater inclination towards a dominance/submission orientation, especially in husband–wife relationships, which gives rise to a strong feeling that there are standards which must be learnt by the children. These are to be taught by didactic statement enforced by punishment (the father is often the ultimate source for enforcement). It should be noticed that the strength of these is directly related to the immediacy of threats to respectability, of which poverty is one of the greatest, imposing as it does an all round strain from which one is tempted to escape by disreputable means. Thirdly, there are a series of practical difficulties: overcrowding, larger families, restricted ability to provide privileges by spending money, more time spent on housework in bad housing in areas where the air pollution is high, and thus less to spend with the children. Strength of character is seen much more in terms of sticking to your guns no matter what the situation than it is in the middle class, although in practice there is probably as much variability in actual treatment of the child as there is in the middle class.

In general middle-class parents see the maintenance of controls over conduct as something growing from an inner anxiety, but which is controlled and adapted to the situation; working-class parents see it as obedience to an overriding certain knowledge of what is right.

Kohn and Carroll[7] give some information about relationships with older children and distinguish between boys and girls (there are only twenty-five sons and twenty-five daughters in this American study, but they did interview both parents and children). This shows that the working-class mothers did not expect their husbands to play any considerable role in dealing with sons or daughters, but when they did they expected them to be directive and positive and to mix encouragement and restraint in carrying it out. Middle-class mothers expected the father to be generally supportive. While working-class mothers were inclined to be critical of their husbands' efforts with sons, the fathers were happy with their restricted roles; whereas middle-class mothers were less critical of their husbands, but the husbands were much more anxious and dissatisfied with their roles. So far as daughters are concerned, the working-class father was not expected to intervene and did not; and the middle-class father took less responsibility.

It has been argued that the working-class boy has more difficulty in identifying with the father as the father only imposes constraints; but there seems to be no reason why the boy should not identify himself in the same role as a source of authority and constraint. It has equally been argued that the middle-class boy does not identify with his father because his time is devoted to the work role; in England it is probable that the prevalence of overtime takes the father out of the home as much as the heavily engrossed businessman or professional. It may well be, however, that the general communication difficulties weigh more heavily in the working-class situation and the father–son relationship is more explosive. Social skills are learned more slowly in the working class, so that even if the father in his age has learned how to handle people, he may not have been very good at this when the children were young. Further, the more authoritarian nature of his role may well lead to serious clashes if he is unreasonable, or in the son's adolescence.

The attachment to 'external' standards may partially account for some of the problems of antisocial behaviour referred to elsewhere.

The framework set up is strong, but if the working-class boy or girl (or adult) breaks through it the fall from grace is all the more complete. 'Respectability', community acceptance and self-respect go together; loss of respectability is liable to put the sinner outside the pale in his own estimation as well as that of others.

The lightening of pressure is quite clearly leading to a more middle-class pattern in the handling of children, and the younger married generation is much less likely to adhere to stringent ideas on standards. It is, however, doubtful whether they have the ability to handle the more fluid and complex internal family relationships which result. It may well be true that the middle-class self-discipline/ social-skill pattern works well in a wide variety of circumstances, but it is not easy to operate, and if badly done, can lead to serious difficulties. The move towards personalising both women and children over the majority of the population is, like comparative affluence, a voyage into an uncharted sea. It is likely to take a generation or two to adjust to the new situation. In the meanwhile the cult of individual personality is likely to lead to excesses, particularly in the young.

The young and the old 7

Most of the argument about teenagers seems to be, implicitly or explicitly, about working-class teenagers; it is probably permissible, therefore, to assume that writings on this subject, unless they specifically say otherwise, have working-class boys and girls in mind.

The great volume of comment and criticism about young people is not matched by the amount of reliable information about them. Much more is known about deviant than about non-deviant adolescents and on any kind of measurement the deviants remain a small proportion. In 1966 the number of appearances in courts followed by a finding of guilt for boys in the fourteen to seventeen age group, although increasing rapidly, still only represented just over 3 per cent of the age group and for the seventeen to twenty-one just under 3 per cent. These may well represent a much higher rate of actual delinquency, and in areas with a heavy concentration of lower working-class people both these rates may be considerably higher; but we are then dealing with the deviant stratum to a much greater extent. In any case, much of this seems to be transitory, as the appearance rate declines in the twenty to thirty age group, and presumably the unreported rate with it. Similarly, the proportion of young people who might by any stretch of the imagination be described as drug addicts, or heavy drinkers, is also very small.

The young are, of course, much more visible at present than they have ever been. To start with, there are more of them, due to high postwar birth rates. They have also benefited a good deal from postwar affluence and since they are less committed, are more often out and about. Firms, selling records and clothes in particular, early began to see that they constituted an important new market and started to create an image of the 'teenager', and this was very much reinforced by the mass media, especially in reporting the activities of the more deviant fringe. Their part was crucial in creating and spreading the 'rock-and-roll' riots of the early 1950s, which in a few countries, particularly Germany, had quite serious effects; and in turning the phrase 'teddy boy' into a term of abuse; and they continue to reinforce the image of a 'teenage culture' which has only a doubtful existence.

Mark Abrams[1] has shown that the element in the fifteen to twenty-four age group's earnings which they spend on themselves rose by 100 per cent between 1938 and 1959. The spending levels and patterns of middle-class and working-class boys, he finds, tend to be much the same (one needs to remember that the middle-class working group is much more depleted by those in further education); but working-class girls have less to spend than their middle-class counterparts. Working-class readers were the main support for publications aimed at this age group, particularly the girls.

The period between school-leaving and marriage has always been one of some strain, and of conflict between conformity and rebellion. This is muted in those who are in further education, where there is more continuity from school to work and a start at a more mature age, and the middle-class assumption of steady upward progress in one's career also tends to affect the perspective. For the working-class adolescent, and particularly for the girls, the comparatively short period between school-leaving and marriage has always been a period of flowering. In the traditional working-class situation, the older girl was much burdened with younger brothers and sisters, and on marriage very soon became overwhelmed by the responsibilities of coping with young children on a very limited income. The situation was not as limited for the boys, but they also realised that marriage would limit their freedom to spend and to go out with the lads. There was thus a general realisation that the teenager should enjoy himself while he could. The extent to which this has been changed in the lower working-class is probably limited, and marriage and children still lead to considerable strain. The situation is less acute in the upper sections of the working class, but the tradition has been strongly reinforced by the factors mentioned above.

There are also some elements in working-class acculturation which, exaggerated in adolescence, tend to support a leisure-based subculture. The tendency to emphasise the importance of physical strength and endurance, still necessary for many jobs, leads to physical forms of self-expression which can easily turn into fighting or vandalism. The flatness of the working-class work career and the consequent emphasis on the search for excitement in leisure supports the belief in 'living for kicks'. The underlying resentment of 'Them' as a reaction to low status leads to acts of defiance and maliciousness, akin to the apparently irrational strikes which abound among the adult men, and the emphasis on unity through solidarity reinforces the natural adolescent tendency towards ganging.

Despite all this, the adolescent generation appear to be a pretty respectable lot. Perhaps the best evidence of this is to be found in Schofield's extremely careful study of sexual experience. A sample survey of 1,873 boys and girls over fifteen and under nineteen shows that of the fifteen to seventeen year-old boys, 11 per cent had experienced sexual intercourse at least once, and 30 per cent of the seventeen to nineteen group, while for the girls, the corresponding figures were 6 per cent and 16 per cent. By cumulation, up to the end of this age period, 34 per cent of all boys and 17 per cent of all girls had had intercourse, the majority after the age of sixteen. Promiscuity was very limited, exactly how limited depends on one's definitions, but the number of sexual partners in the last year of the period is probably the best indication: 12 per cent of the boys and 2 per cent of the girls had more than one sexual partner in the last year, but only 6 per cent of the boys and a very small number of girls had four or more partners in the last year.

There are a number of analyses in Schofield by social class (R.G.s occupational classes I–V). These show no significant differences between the manual and non-manual classes in the proportion experiencing sexual intercourse either in boys or in girls, although there is a slight tendency to a higher rate in working-class boys, more so, oddly enough, in the skilled than the other strata. The only significant difference is, in fact, that middle-class girls more often have experiences falling short of actual intercourse. In terms of the progression from no contact through increasing sex play to intercourse, there was a tendency for the working-class boys to progress more rapidly to intercourse and therefore, to start earlier.[2]

There is not much evidence of a general feeling of relative deprivation amongst British teenagers. Musgrove and Carter[3] both show that their aspirations are quite realistic in the great majority of cases; and Musgrove also finds that it is not the adolescents who reject adults but adults who have a low opinion of adolescents. There may be some truth in the contention of Merton[4] and his followers,[5] that, for the working class, access to cultural goals is blocked by impediments in the social structure (particularly educational impediments), and that this leads to social problems, particularly crime; but the pattern seems to be primarily one of leisure-oriented drift, with an admixture of deviants derived largely from failures in the home.

Unlike the situation in the United States, British teenagers are, despite their growing numbers, in short supply owing to the acute manpower shortage. They have more to spend, they are taller, heavier, and better fed than in the past, and, except for a high rate of motor-cycle accidents,[6] they have very low mortality and morbidity rates. They are increasingly taking part in socially approved activities from religion to youth clubs. The information about clubs is fragmentary and mostly fails to take into account their availability (which varies enormously), and experience over a period; if one looks at a well provided area like Bethnal Green, one finds that the great majority had been club members at some time.[7] Nevertheless working-class boys and girls are less interested in clubs and other 'approved' activities than the middle class. The Crowther Report found that boys who had attended modern schools spent an average of 4·5 evenings per week on leisure activities outside the home as compared with 4·0 for those who had attended grammar and technical schools and spent rather more time on outdoor activities and the cinema. With the girls the patterns were more similar. In general those who took part in further education went to the cinema less. In the grammar and technical school sample 79 per cent of the boys and 60 per cent of the girls were members of one or more clubs at the time of interview, while the corresponding figures for modern schools was 56 per cent and 35 per cent. The samples covered those who had left school eighteen months to three years previously, and because of varying leaving ages covered people from sixteen to over twenty.[8]

In the lower stratum, relative deprivation still exists, and the fragmentation of the working-class tradition has combined with it to create pressures which strongly affect the adolescent population. Lower stratum adolescents are probably not themselves strongly affected by the failure of the educational system to enlist their interests, but they are certainly affected by their inability to live up to the teenage image, through poverty and lack of social skills. Thus the elements of the Mertonian conflict are more evident here, and are combined with the emphases of the acculturation process, noted above, at their strongest, and with the presence of a higher proportion of deviants. The problems of adolescence are thus much accentuated, and it is not surprising that the indices of social strain therefore show substantial increases in recent years.

The old

The Registrar General's most recent projections of population in England and Wales shows an increase in men over sixty-five and women over sixty from 7,400,000 in mid-1966 to 8,900,000 in 1991; the figure for 2001 shows a slight decline, although the total population continues to rise. Since the drop in mortality rates for women has been much more dramatic than for men, the proportion of surviving women will increase. What proportion would be comprised in any specific definition of the working class is difficult, if not impossible, to say; although so far as public provision is concerned, it is likely that most of it will be for working-class people.

The considerable increase in concern for old people, and in public provision in the period since 1945, should not lead us into too much overemphasis concerning the problems of the aged. The suggestion that old people were being abandoned by their families was effectively scotched by the work of the Institute of Community Studies.[9] Family structure in the working class has been discussed already, and it is clear from this that although distances may increase as transport becomes easier, the majority of the elderly are cared for by their children, who try to see that they remain within reach. Increasing long distance mobility may, however, cause problems, since old people are reluctant to move.

The chief problem arises from the fact that the present generation of old people, whose children were born in the 1920s and 1930s had fewer children than those whose main child-bearing period was before the First World War or after the Second, so that there are proportionately more of them, with fewer children to cope, and a greater likelihood of childlessness; and of spinsterhood since the holocaust of 1914–18 removed many potential husbands. They may also be suffering from the penalties of improved health services, which keep them alive for longer periods, but often frail or bed-ridden; these same services also keep them sprightly longer, and it is difficult to say whether the total outcome is more or less dependency.

It is very clear from Townsend's work and from studies of the long term populations of psychiatric hospitals and chronic sick wards that the major problem is those old people who have no family or have become detached from their families. Townsend[10] shows that the major reason for entry into old people's homes is not incapacity but lack of anyone to provide an alternative and Wedderburn and the Government Enquiry[11] demonstrate that the worst off are single and widowed women, who are not only most often without support from relatives, but are the poorest. The oldest age groups are all worse off than the younger, again partly due to loss of husbands or children, but also due to lower income. Some of the material in *The Last Refuge* indicates also the effects of increased geographical and social mobility. Indeed, poverty is widespread among the old and particularly amongst those of working class origins. About half of the sample of 3,146 income units in 1962 had income levels at or about the current subsistence rate, and Wedderburn, the Government Enquiry, and the Allen Committee[12] found that about ten per cent of households with retired heads were entitled to National Assistance but not getting it. Since then the introduction of the supplementary benefit scheme and increases in the basic rates have probably improved the position, although by how much is not yet clear. The levels adopted are, however, very low in terms of current incomes, and even if there are less in real hardship (and Wedderburn suggested these amounted to about 5 per cent) income is still very low for a substantial part of the elderly population.

These authors also investigated the amount of assistance given by social services in the community. It was found that 11·8 per cent of all old people were receiving at least one domicilary service in 1962; but while 15·4 per cent of those classified as skilled manual were getting the services, only 12·9 per cent of the semiskilled and 12·6 per cent of the unskilled were getting them. It is not known what is the extent of the services given to different groups, for example, in terms of time, or numbers of visits. An assessment of unmet needs of those living in the community showed that there were substantial deficiencies in the provision for home helps, meals on wheels, chiropody, services connected with hearing and sight, contact with G.P.s and the provision of sheltered housing. In respect of the last, it was calculated that at least 5 per cent of the elderly population in the community needed to be accommodated in sheltered housing, and perhaps as many again amongst those now in institutions.

The differential effects of social class are clearly seen in *The Last Refuge*. While there was not much difference in the proportions from various classes in the sample of admissions, bad housing more often sent them in. The population of ex-public assistance institutions was heavily weighted with former manual workers, and especially the unskilled. Some local authorities took the view that many of them, especially the old men, were too rough and unpleasant in their habits to be accommodated in a more recently built home. As a result 40 per cent of all men in former workhouses were in social class V. Once in the institution, the data suggests that former manual workers were less often visited (possibly because they were more often isolated), and were more inclined to resignation with their lot.

In sum, the strong kinship basis of working-class life tends to provide and care for old people, but even if there were no other factors, the characteristics of the present older generation would still leave many of them without this cover. Increasing mobility, rehousing policies which pay no attention to the need to care for old people, and the pressures of poverty, bad housing and incapacity, tend to produce a crop of difficult problems for the public services. It seems likely that many of these problems will ease off in about thirty to forty years time, but in the meanwhile, they are likely to prove a great trial. The immense financial burden of pensions (currently about £1,300 m) makes governments wary of increasing them; while the administrative difficulties of what has now come to be politely called 'selectivity' makes it very difficult to operate fairly and without stigma. At the time of writing no real improvement in the public provision for working-class old people seems likely in the immediate future, and the best hope lies in that part of the working class which really is increasing in affluence, and can supplement the public services both in money and care.

There are a number of other aspects of ageing which could be discussed, but perhaps the most relevant are questions concerned with work and retirement. The general pattern is that for the most part, the majority of men need to retire between sixty and seventy-five. Of all men living beyond seventy-five only some 13 per cent are recorded as being at work, and they are mainly in a comparatively few jobs such as farm, garden and factory labourers, watchmen and personal service workers, all presumably on light work. Non-manual grades show a considerably higher proportion still at work, but it is difficult to say how far many of these people, though still reporting themselves as working in a trade or profession, actually do anything.[13]

By the age of sixty-five, Le Gros Clark estimates that 15–20 per cent of all manual workers had moved to less exacting work or should have done so, and a continuing decline in capacity was apparent; most obviously in heavy manual work. Perhaps another 10 per cent or so suffered already from incapacitating illness. Because of the natural decline in capacity, which not only affects physical strength but also capacity to work at speed or under pressure, the degree to which old people can continue to be employed depends greatly on the possibility of redeployment. It seems clear that a number of men do change jobs after the age of fifty-five. As one would conclude from

7

the morbidity figures for miners, there is a considerable movement away from face work to surface work; but mining is a rapidly declining sector. The total movement, as estimated by Clark, seems very low, and nowhere near the 30–40 per cent he suggests should move—but the figures he is working on are out of date, and it is difficult to say whether there have been recent improvements.

This seems unlikely, because the increasing degree of emphasis on flow production, in which the whole of the process is dependent upon steady rates of flow in its parts, militates against the employment of the older person, who is more likely to be absent and less likely to be able to keep up, and to take rapid action when there is a disturbance in the flow. Furthermore, his work is apt to be measured against a costed output-per-man based on work study, and he is not likely to come well out of the comparison. Increases in shift work, to keep machinery going, are also not likely to recommend themselves to older men. It is true that there are a number of 'light' jobs in all factories, but it seems unlikely that these are anything like enough for the number of men who need to change, and they need to be shared with the convalescent younger man and with the disabled. Even the job of watchman or gatekeeper is sometimes combined with others, such as security or fireman, and thus regarded as a younger man's job.

It is not likely that automation, strictly defined, will become very general in industry in the near future, but in so far as this may mean employing a number of key operatives whose job is to watch and operate a series of important controls, there are obvious dangers in employing older men, who might suffer more easily from mental fatigue. On the other hand, the growth of service industries and the need for 'jobbing' maintenance work on a small scale, may open up fields for older men, if younger ones are increasingly unavailable.

Leisure 8

In the fifteen years between 1951 and 1966, the average working week in the United Kingdom fell by four hours from 44·6 to 40·7, and the average hours actually worked by two hours only from 46·3 to 44·3.[1] This exemplifies both the gradual move towards increased leisure and the persistence in Britain of the tradition of overtime. Overtime is probably worked mainly by younger men, particularly young married men and by those with low wages, if they can get it.

It would not be accurate to conclude that the rest of the worker's time is leisure. Much of it must obviously be devoted to sleep and food, and there is also a good deal of time which is taken up in carrying out chores. The working housewife probably has little real leisure if this means time in which she can do what she likes, but one might equally say that the non-working housewife with several children and limited help also has very little leisure time. In addition some activities have both work and leisure content, for example, going down to the corner shop and buying groceries while chatting to the owner and other acquaintances; for those who like it, repainting the house. Thus leisure time and activities are difficult to define precisely. Nevertheless, some things—going to the pictures or the club—are clearly leisure and can be measured. Unfortunately we do not have much easily accessible factual information about leisure in Britain, and most of the information available is related to adolescents. Adolescent leisure has been dealt with in chapter 7. Here we deal with the subject in more general terms.

S. de Grazia[2] has brought together a good deal of information relating to the United States. An analysis of a national sample of 5,000 were asked what they did yesterday; this is given for people over twenty and analysed by educational attainment. There are distinct gradients moving up the scale in those who read magazines or books, listened to records, went to meetings or went pleasure driving, but otherwise there is little variation. Those with the least education score were highest on the item 'none of those listed', but whether this is a 'not known' category is not apparent. People seemed to watch television or work around the house or garden just as much, whatever their level of education. Viewing studies in England also show little variation in the time spent viewing, although the actual programmes and whether viewing BBC or ITV are affected by class.

Himmelweit *et al.*[3] in a study of 4,500 children aged 10–11 and 13–14 in 1955–56, found that intelligence, personality and parental pressures were more important than class in their effect on viewing habits. More difficult family situations, combined with a mainly passive reaction, put up the amount and effect of viewing time. An interesting point is that the younger and duller children benefited more, since they received a lot of information in dramatic form, which otherwise would probably not have impressed them. How far this might be applicable to the duller adults at the bottom of the working class is an interesting question. An analysis of programmes for adults in play form, including serials, showed that they portrayed substantially an urban upper-middle or middle-class society; but since this time there has been some move towards working-class settings, of which *Coronation Street* is the most popular. It probably remains true that in general the content is more often middle- than working-class. It is not surprising, however, that fantasy heroes live in fantasy backgrounds rather than a two up and two down. 'People like us' are not part of the heroic tradition.

Mass culture

This leads us to consider what is often described as 'mass culture'. Discussions under this heading tend to be both confused and heavily biased. The bias is easy to explain, as it depends upon how far one sees 'high' culture as the best that is available, or alternatively how far one is committed to proletarian views in which the 'people' should spontaneously produce and develop their own culture which is, for this reason, intrinsically best. The confusion derives from the difficulty of defining 'best', and the fact that some of the argument is about curtailment of freedom of choice, some of it about the effects of money-making versus education in its widest sense, and some about the value of participation.

H. J. Gans, in a very useful recent article,[4] summarises the accusations against mass culture. It is mass-produced by the profit-minded and it panders to the worst in ourselves rather than the best; it borrows from high culture and debases it; it lures away those who might otherwise be really creative with offers of large sums; it spreads a low level of culture and thus society becomes less civilised; and it helps demagogues to appeal to the worst instincts, and thus threatens democracy.

In discussing these it is necessary to say first that all the evidence shows that for the most part what people want is entertainment, and that they treat it as entertainment, and thus as peripheral to their lives. It is probable that those who are strongly attached to high culture, who are a small minority in the population, obtain deeper satisfactions and that it is less peripheral to them, but it is only of major importance for a very few outside those who are actually engaged in producing it. If there are any effects, they are mainly in general terms of habituating people to, say, scenes of violence; but even this is difficult to assess because habituation itself dulls the senses. The ritual western, though normally extremely violent, is hardly registered as such unless it departs from the norm in some way, for example by showing torture realistically. It is then more likely to be shocking and distasteful than to be enjoyable.

It is thus difficult to believe in accusations of serious damage, and the worst one can say is that mass culture is superficial. The fact that it is highly industrialised does not necessarily mean that it is transmitting things which are undesirable, or even restricting the creative spirit. Much of mass culture is very secondhand in that it ultimately depends upon not what its immediate producers think of the tastes of their audience, but what they think their advertisers think about their tastes, the result being a lowest common multiple.

Ultimately it is true that the public gets what it wants, but it might have wanted something else if it had been offered.

In fact, much of high culture is highly organised and very dependent on what taste leaders—the Arts Council, publishers, impresarios—think their public wants; and they might have preferred something else. They are, however, much less bombarded with advertising and are presumably more sure where their own tastes lie; it is easier to kill things they do not like by failing to support them.

As to borrowing and debasing high culture, this may be true, but it seems unlikely that any of the creators are harmed, and some are maintained on it (Mozart and Schubert might have lived longer and produced more with the royalties from even one or two of their most popular songs).

There is a false opposition in all these arguments: that there are only two cultures, high culture and mass culture. Gans distinguishes six taste cultures: creator high culture which consists of the artistic world and its critics, and a select public which is aesthetically knowledgeable; it is based largely on exclusiveness and dislikes anything which becomes widely popular. Consumer-oriented high culture draws on the same content but more selectively and less creatively, and distributes it to the wider public who read the culture-conscious magazines and have feelings and opinions about aesthetics. Upper-middle culture is the main support of the 'better' plays, films, novels and music, though the patrons do not see themselves as intellectuals, but as well informed practical people. Lower-middle culture is the major audience for those who produce the best sellers, the Hollywood spectacular, the domestic drama and situational comedy, and the prints of Van Gogh minus ear, and flying geese. They tend in terms of high culture to be in the last generation, and they reject most of present-day high culture.

Lower culture is the main working-class culture. It stresses concrete situations, and plot rather than ideas, simple conflicts of good and evil and the *Coronation Street* type of serial. There is rather more division of content between what is liked by men and by women, consistent with the stronger division between the life styles of the sexes. It emphasises performers and stars. It likes gossip with human interest and vivid presentation. It is rather against most of high culture and also against realistic description or representation of sexuality, but it likes the less subtle sex jokes and the lavatory joke. Lower-lower culture magnifies most of these traits, and likes its material even more simply laid out in captioned pictures, or short features and it is even more given on the male side to the violent and active, and on the female to the sentimental and romantic.

It is obvious that these are defined largely in class terms and related to the characteristics of each class. The important point is that they represent referent areas within which standards of good and bad are judged. Furthermore, it is possible to move up or down to the next stratum in a kind of taste mobility which may well follow social mobility. The practical conclusion is that reached by the Royal Commission on Broadcasting; that one needs to provide a range from which people can choose so that they can move 'up' if they want to. The condemnation of the profit-centred culture merchant is that he fails to provide these avenues.

The growth of the mass media, as Whannel and Hall[5] point out, has been associated with a considerable increase in personalisation. The success of the large circulation newspapers is closely related to their style of presentation, which not only includes gossip columns, but tends to turn everything into gossip. Thus, if there is any way of personalising an event by describing it in terms of social behaviour or relationships, it is presented in this way. The most successful of the dailies, the *Daily Mirror*, is always gossipy, matey, and even when truculent does its best to sound like the forthright, no-nonsense man expounding his views. Similarly a number of very successful television and radio programmes are based upon the idea that one is looking over the shoulders of ordinary families, though the above authors make the point that some of the most successful of these (*Steptoe and Son*, *Meet the Wife*, *Till Death Do Us Part*), gain from a sufficient exaggeration and contrast of working-class characters to introduce both humour and strains into the relationships shown.

An interest in gossip is by no means confined to the working class. Raymond Williams[6] gives figures showing that the leading daily paper

95

of the better off is not *The Times* or even the *Daily Telegraph*, but the *Daily Express*. The fact that the *Mirror* is very firmly rooted in working-class readership and the *Express* provides more for the upper class, gives a different tang to the way in which gossip and news is presented. The *Express* is more snobbish, and more given to righteous indignation, while the *Mirror* is more human interest and 'come off it'.

On the whole the type of material heavily consumed by the British working class reflects the tastes of the respectable, married, skilled or semiskilled worker. Situations and plots tend to be sentimentalised for the women, and fast-moving for the men. There is little subtlety of characterisation or of deeply felt emotional relationships between people, since this is something which causes discomfort, as does any real attempt at sexual accuracy. Humour is broad and rather cocky, with catch phrases or actions; music is sentimental or tuneful rather than 'pop'.

The question arises, where do we go next? The excesses of the adolescent pop and magazine world have as yet had little effect on the newspapers, but rather more on the other entertainment media, where some of the nicer boys (the Beatles, Tommy Steele) have become family favourites. This public, however, really prefers Ken Dodd, both as a comedian and as singer of sentimental ballads.

Sport

The amount of really useful information about sport is very limited. We do not, for instance, know the stratification analysis of those who take part in, or watch regularly, different kinds of sport. Football matches, for instance, regularly draw large crowds, but whether they are representative of all social classes is not clear. There are undoubtedly some very specialised upper-class sports like polo, which are exclusive on the score of the equipment needed, let alone membership of élite clubs. Golf has been in this category but is probably obtaining a wider membership, though remaining a middle-class sport. Boxing seems to be declining, especially in its professional form, which now probably attracts the lower stratum of the working class. Television, oddly enough, has popularised both the theatrical antics of all-in wrestling, and the upper-class sport of horse-jumping, but it is likely from its popularity on ITV that the former is much more the working-class choice. Motor car and cycle racing have also benefited greatly from TV. Wireless, TV and the ability to pay both to travel to matches and to see them, has led to considerable dependence upon mass support, mainly from the working class. As a wider section, especially of younger people, are able to afford equipment, there is likely to be an increasing demand for those sports which are reasonably easy to provide for in parks and recreation grounds, and for swimming baths. There is much complaint about non-participation in sport, but most large urban authorities cannot meet the present demand.

Formal organisations

The small amount of academic work under this heading shows that working-class people are proportionately less often members of clubs than the middle class, but much depends on the type of organisation and the stratum within the working class at which we are looking. It is probably true that the membership of social clubs is not high amongst the unskilled and it is likely that the solid core of clubs in membership with the Working Men's Club and Institute Union is skilled and semiskilled. Much depends on local conditions, and there are many areas where the Miners' Welfare, or the British Legion is the general club for a small town or village. In Ashton, however, the Miners' Welfare was not well patronised and there were six other clubs with a membership half as large again as the male population. They seemed to operate as rather good class pubs, offering not only the bar, around which most activity centred, but also the weekend concert (at the three largest) featuring paid 'turns'. There were also housey-housey (now renamed 'Bingo') sessions, and equipment for billiards, darts and other games. In Ashton, billiards and snooker had declined, but whether this is general is not clear; the Working Men's Club and Institute Union runs annual area and national competitions for billiards, snooker and darts, and, in 1966, 266 clubs and 4,928 players took part, team darts apparently being the most popular, the entry of 239 teams having doubled in the last seven years. The Ashton club also had a number of internal associations, one of which was the Angling Club, another activity for which the Union runs competitions. Another association ran coach tours.

The number of clubs belonging to the Union, and the membership, have increased almost without check since the Union was founded in 1887, and at the end of 1966 there were 3,813 clubs with over 3 million members. While it remains true that this is largely a male activity, there are 600,000 women members and 2,735 of the clubs admit women to membership. Since working-class women do not normally join clubs—and they differ here from their middle-class counterparts who more often do so, and who tend to form the backbone of the Women's Institutes, the Townswomen's Guilds and even more the WRVS—it is probable that these are largely subsidiary to male memberships in the form of wives and girl friends joining, but they do demonstrate a movement away from the exclusive men's club, which parallels developments in the upper-class club of this type.

Outside these clubs there are many small organisations based on sports and hobbies, often centring round a pub. The decline of the little slum pub at the end of the street is probably removing one of the major social centres; and the big new pubs serving a large area cannot be used in the same way.

Gambling clubs have proliferated since the Betting, Gaming and Lotteries Act 1963 which left very profitable loopholes in the gaming laws. The main growth has apparently been in provincial towns, especially in the North, but it is not clear how far they are patronised by the working class, and they are probably a peripheral activity with a high proportion of deviants. They are about to be brought under control. The Betting Shop, which was the main result of the Act, is prevented by law from having any characteristics of a club, but nevertheless provides an informal meeting place for the more earnest punters. Bingo Clubs provide a somewhat similar and more respectable gambling service, for housewives in particular—though not confined to them—and in a number of them there is some attempt to produce a club atmosphere.

The important thing about working-class club memberships, as Klein points out, is that they are highly concentrated in organisations which are totally working class. Bottomore, studying a small country town,[7] found that manual and non-manual workers did, in fact, belong to the same clubs, but that there was a strong tendency to separation in clubs centred round different types of activity, and to segregation within the clubs of mixed membership, including an almost universal concentration of leadership in the middle classes. In Banbury this situation was further complicated by religious and party differences, and the native/outsider split. Not giving yourself airs or putting yourself above others has already been commented on as an important value; and the solution in terms of associational hierarchies is either to leave leadership to the stuck-up people who enjoy it, or to reduce the degree of formality.

The ' Binge'

Hoggart and other writers have commented upon the way in which leisure is enjoyed, and particularly the release of tensions in the wholehearted 'binge'. The deprivations of traditional working-class life put a premium on enjoying to the full the day or night out, Saturday night at the pub, and the more ritual occasions of weddings and Christmas. Considerable amounts, and sometimes more than can really be afforded, are spent on these occasions, particularly in ensuring that there is a plentiful supply of beer, and something a bit more refined for the ladies—traditionally port.

'Binges' on special occasions are, of course, common to all classes, and the particular character of the working-class 'binge' is probably more apparent in the lower half of the working class. There is a great deal of noise (but working-class households are usually pretty noisy with radio or television going most of the time and people talking over it); much interchange of jokes, the crudity of which rapidly increases as one moves down the scale, a general slight drunkenness with some of the men rather worse for wear (somebody is nearly always sick); loud singing, generally of popular ballads (the amateur pub singer and parties are still common in working-class areas, but some pubs employ professional groups). There is not much dancing in the older groups who are not very much at home with it, though the younger ones are—but this often depends on the space available and it is not usually possible in small houses or pubs. Fish and chips is the traditional meal for a day out, or after an evening in the pub; it is still the cheapest and most nourishing meal you can buy anywhere—you can get very little even in a cheap café for less than two shillings.

The village magico-religious festival has virtually disappeared, but remains in some smaller places in a variety of local guises, some of them of very ancient derivation. Occasions such as the Manchester Whit Walks, consisting of two processions through the town on different days, one for Protestants and one for Catholics, still provide for the appetite for pageantry and ceremony, but outside London, there is little opportunity to indulge this. Oddly enough, student rag processions have tended to provide something of an alternative, but without the general holiday which was the concomitant of the feast day. There is, in fact, a distinct dearth of 'occasions' upon which everybody can turn out and cheer, something much enjoyed at one time in working-class communities. The football match Saturday, complete with pub crawl, is a largely male substitute, and the women have lost out most on this.

In general, the release of pressure from hardship, and the more general availability of leisure and the means to enjoy it has rather tended to destroy the 'binge' in its traditional working-class form. The creeping onset of education, sophistication and the middle-class type of respectability all work against letting your hair down in an uninhibited way. It must be reported, with a tinge of melancholy, that 'Knees Up Mother Brown' is disappearing even faster than the charladies who are traditionally reputed to be its most active performers.

The outstanding quality of the poverty stricken must be endurance, and this leads not only to resignation in this life, but to expectations that there must be a compensating justice somewhere, probably after death.

As Seabrook says:

Resignation characterised their attitude to life and they were only sustained by an uncontestable belief in some fundamental though unrevealed cosmic justice. 'It was sent.' And they believed that the life of each individual is made up of an equal amount of hardship, joy, suffering, pleasure. The ostensible disparity between the lives of people merely indicated the submerged nature of those equalising factors they knew to exist. Justice will always be established sooner or later, wrong always atoned for, good inevitably rewarded (*The Unprivileged*, p. 30).

The comforts of religion have a special value in this situation, but religious values are one thing, and religious organisations another. The emergence of the industrial working class in Britain in the early nineteenth century, in common with the growth of the middle class and of the ethic of capitalism earlier, was accompanied and supported by a new religious departure, the growth of nonconformity. Methodism, swept out of the hands of the Wesleys by the needs of the displaced and disoriented urban working class, presented them with a structure which was not, at least originally, associated with the bosses; which was uplifting; and which unlike the more Calvinistic types of Protestantism where salvation was assigned to the successful few, offered wider hopes in the after life. It soon came, also, to offer a strongly ordered and democratic structure which could be entered and supported without belonging to the establishment.

The gradual assertion of working class rights, especially through unionism, and the capability of the establishment in absorbing, if slowly, the need for a changed outlook; together with the institutionalisation of the nonconformist churches and their greater identification with the upper working class, and the successful entrepreneurs, greatly reduced the gap. Anglican evangelicalism also had some success. The lower working class showed little tendency to evolve brotherhood sects, as have other oppressed classes, but tended rather to accept a general religiosity, based on Christianity, but extracting very largely the more comforting doctrines of a world order ordained by God, beyond understanding, which decreed sufferings which had to be accepted with fatalism, for which there would be compensations in an afterlife. Linked with this was a continuance of the long rustic tradition of magical rites embodied in a list of superstitions based on animism and the pervading pressure of evil spirits.

The advent of the Irish navvy increased the lower working class Catholic element. They had a much stronger communal feeling, and the Catholic Church remained a stronger influence, notably in the area of fertility, a belief which echoed the heavy emphasis upon virility of the unskilled worker.

Since the turn of the century, participation in church and denominational activities has declined, the change showing itself in a steady drop in the proportions baptised and confirmed. The sense of occasion which ceremony enhances has maintained the role of church and chapel in marriage and burial, but the relevance of these as religious occasions seems small.

Unfortunately, we have no very useful statistical information about religious activity or belief, but it seems likely that the upper working class are nearer to the middle class in associating religious conformity with respectability; sending their children dutifully to Sunday School; and attending church themselves; although this applies to a minority. Gorer's figures[1] are based on claimed class and therefore reflect status aspirations; and they are also from written answers to questionnaires which means they underrepresent the less literate (not to mention those who did not read *The People* in 1951). The figures show in all classes much greater belief and religious activity amongst women than men, amongst the old than the young, and outside the big towns. There are fewer non-believers amongst those who claim to be working class. Of those who accept membership of a religious organisation, the Church of England appears to be spread out fairly evenly, but weaker in the north where the R.C.s and Methodists are stronger. This is allied to the working–class affiliation of these two faiths. Those who go to church regularly at least once a week, form about a sixth of the population, but this seems to be heavily weighted with under-eighteens, the upper middle class, women, and small town and village dwellers; 48 per cent of the men and 31 per cent of the women never go to church, or only for weddings and funerals, and this seems to be the major pattern in the working class. On the other hand, those who claim to be working-class seem to follow a pattern of teaching children to say a prayer, and sending them to Sunday School, but this presumably has little effect on adult participation or belief. The method by which the information was collected may well have biased these figures.

The general trend of the few figures we have, if we exclude R.C.s, show a steady decline in activity from top to bottom, and a general decline throughout the whole of British society. The meaning of these, however, is more difficult to assess since church activity does not necessarily mean that the church is playing any considerable part in people's lives. Wilson,[2] comparing Britain and the United States points out that while church activity is very high in the latter, it is the result of the way in which the churches have grown up in that country, and the actual degree of secularisation seems to be as great as in Britain. Many of those things the churches and chapels offered; comfort, care for social casualties, the excitement of high days and holidays, are now provided by other means. One might think that the greater need for consolation, and the smaller degree of penetration of rational living which characterises the lower working class would offer more scope to religious activity, but this is an area where pentecostal and revivalist sects are more appropriate, and the Englishman's strong dislike for emotional display makes it impossible for them to gain a hold. It may be that affluence and its accompanying respectability will lead to a revival of church based activity, but the competition faced by the church is greater than ever before.

Politics

It has become something of a stereotyped reaction since World War II to identify working-class interests with the Labour Party, and middle-class interests with the Conservative Party. It is, of course true, that the Labour Party grew out of the trade union movement at the beginning of the century and has continued to find its main support, particularly in terms of money, in the unions, and in this sense it has tended much more to try to identify itself with the interests of the working man. This concern has not been reciprocated for most of the period since the Labour Party became a force in British Politics. Between the wars the Conservatives, either alone or in coalition, were in power solidly except for short intermissions of Labour government in 1924 and 1929–31; and the coalition which followed the 1931 crisis and lasted until 1935 was rejected by the Parliamentary Labour Party but heavily supported by voters of all classes. Indeed since 1918, when Labour began to be a real political force, the Conservatives and their coalitions have had clear majorities in eight out of the fourteen elections and the Labour Party have had very shaky majorities in four of their six victories. Thus, while it is true that the Labour Party has more wasted votes because of large majorities, in fact, substantial proportions of the working class have not voted Labour in all the elections; even in 1945 about a third of those identified by the Gallup Poll as working-class or very poor voted Conservative[3] and there appears to be a fairly consistent pattern of 30–40 per cent Conservative voting amongst the manual electorate.

Part of the difficulty, of course, rests in the definition of class by occupation. A National Opinion Poll Survey conducted just before the 1964 election showed considerable differences between claimed class and class measured by occupation, and a stronger tendency for this to happen in the working class than the middle class[4]; and Runciman has shown that self rated class makes a substantial difference in party preference.[5] He agrees with other studies that women and older voters in the working class are more likely to vote Conservative; not, as might be expected, the high income skilled workers. Indeed, the major constituent of the working-class Conservative vote in recent years seems to be the poorer and older women, although there is also an element of manual workers and their wives who appear to identify themselves with the middle class as a normative reference group, and thus vote Conservative.

The former type of voting is often called 'deferential' since it is based upon the assumption that 'They' know best, and are best fitted to govern. It is doubtful if this term really applies in its full sense, since manual workers, even more than other people, are inclined to see governments and politicians as remote, and as the Gallup Poll shows, have very little knowledge of what they are doing or even who they are. A survey made in 1960 showed only 15 per cent claiming to be very interested in politics, and despite the 1959 election, less than half the 21 per cent of men claiming to be very interested in politics had attended a political meeting in the last year. These results show a lower proportion of working than middle class claiming an interest.

Despite the minority in the working class who manage to turn the scales against the Labour Party, British political allegiances show rather more consistent class trends than are found in Australia, Canada, or the United States. One of Mark Abrams's findings is that respondents do not recognise policies clearly but are pretty clear that the Conservatives stand for the middle class and Labour for the working class. Alford,[6] comparing Britain with the countries listed above, finds that voting studies and performance show a much more solid and steady class allegiance; overriding other possible sectional interests. In Australia, a Catholic party has arisen mainly on the issue of anti-communism and has been able to amass sufficient support to cause the Labour Party to lose several elections. In the U.S.A. while there is a general tendency for Labour to support the

Democrats, this is so overlaid by the variety of other issues which arise from a very large and diversified population, that it is not a dominant feature; while in Canada regional and religious differences are much more important than class.

However, Alford's comparison between a small and unified country like Britain and these much larger federal countries is bound to bring out the importance of regional differences in the latter. It is extremely difficult to find a comparable situation. In West Germany there is a strong religious split; in Norway the party allegiances form along farm versus town populations; in Japan deferential and interest based agrarian and business voters provide a continuing two-thirds majority for the Conservatives while the Socialists consist of middle- and lower-middle left-wing 'intellectuals'; in New Zealand the rural/urban split is again evident. There are few countries where urbanisation has gone as far as it has in Britain, and where the historical development of government has produced anything like the even balance between the unified radical and conservative political groupings.

So far as policy is concerned, it is doubtful whether the working class has ever had a strong identification with the Labour Party. In the early days, the Party undoubtedly represented a minority who would stick up for the rights of the working man, but its interwar socialist policies probably found little response in the working class in general, who preferred deferential or charismatic voting. Labour's postwar nationalisation programme also probably meant very little, but its identification with a vigorous postwar policy of welfare measures has had much more impact.

Studies of voting allegiance, however, do not attach much importance to policy issues, nor to the quality of candidates, nor party organisation. Party allegiance seems to be built up largely through an acculturation process in which voters tend to follow their Dads. In recent years also, the equality of support for the two major parties means that many comparatively small variations are likely to decide an election. Complex changes in age and sex groupings in constituencies; the effects of resentment at some action of the Government or general disappointment or lack of interest in its performance; the comparative charisma of party leaders; even the weather on election day may have some effect. We also appear to be back in the interwar situation where everyone knows what is wrong but nobody knows how to put it right. Thus successive administrations come in on a limited tide of enthusiasm (just enough to tip the balance) for the belief that they can now succeed where the others failed; and after a time are dismissed partly because they are equally helpless, and partly because nothing effective can be done without upsetting large numbers of voters.

It is not at all clear how the changes which are likely to take place within the working class will affect voting. The older deferential voter is probably dying off, but there is some growth of manual workers with strong middle-class identification, who have become sufficiently individualistic and aspirant to eschew the traditional Labour Party identification. The gradual disappearance of the proletarian type of community with strong working-class consciousness is matched by the dissolution of the specifically socialist cast of mind of the Labour Party, so that it represents rather more of a party of change associated particularly with collective action on the welfare front, as against the literally more conservative and more individualistic cast of mind of their opponents.

So far, upward mobility through the educational system seems to have had little impact. Studies of students are doubtfully indicative of future voting behaviour, but they seem to show a move to the right in those from manual worker parents. Rather more work needs to be done to establish whether this trend really affects voting behaviour, or whether it is merely part of the general move towards consensus which has been taking place in British political opinion. If, however, social mobility really reduces both left- and right-wing extremism, it may well be that the number of the uncommitted will slowly rise, thus returning to British politics a degree of fluidity it appears to have lost.

Religion and politics

These two subjects have been put together in one chapter purely for convenience. There is, however, a complex relationship between the two which could be explored in relation to the working class; but the subject is not an easy one nor is there any summarised reading matter. It has been thought better, therefore, not to tackle this particular area.

Deviance

It is not, of course, possible to discuss in detail here the numerous forms which deviance may take. We can only talk briefly about the deviant stratum, and about a few major problems.

Probably the best short description of the deviant stratum is to be found in the Radby study. Although it refers only to twenty-five families in a small town, by multiplication it could be transferred to any large town. Some of these families come under the heading of problem families, and these are described in more detail by both Harriet Wilson and A. F. Philp;[1] there are also many who live in much the same way, but without the complex difficulties which bring them into the problem family classification. A summary of a number of these studies is available in Klein's book.

The major characteristic of this stratum and the reason for its rejection by the majority of the working class is that it has little interest in respectability. Homes are squalid, badly equipped, unrepaired; clothing is unwashed, inadequate and torn or flashy and tawdry; children are undisciplined, uncared for, and often dressed in ill-fitting cast-offs; meals are sketchy, and may never be taken at a table, often because there is no cutlery; food stands about and is wasted; there is no proper storage space for anything, and things lie about—food, clothing, all mixed up with buckets of dirty water and sometimes urine, since the lavatories are constantly blocked.

The men appear and disappear, sometimes in work, sometimes not, but it does not follow that they are all unemployed or thieves, or that the household income is noticeably less than many of the more respectable lower working class. Indeed, since these families are often large, there may be several earners and a good deal of money available; but although expensive clothes, bits of furniture, or toys appear from time to time they are soon dilapidated or broken, and new ones are then bought. Things are often acquired expensively on hire purchase or through 'clubs'; the payments are not kept up and they are repossessed.

Relationships become extremely involved because there is a constant interchange of partners. The husband goes off with someone, and another man takes his place; some of the children are legitimate, some illegitimate. The household contains people who may or may not be relatives, and the outsider may be given varying explanations at different times. Extraordinary complications occur, as when the illegitimate child of a young daughter is brought up in the belief that his mother is his older sister, and all his other relationships thus become distorted.

No attempt is made either to hide or explain these turnabouts to children, who also witness the violent quarrels which they cause. The children are pushed out in the street early, and are constantly given money, where there is enough, to get rid of them, so that they eat sweets most of the time. They soon learn in the street and at home that the rule for survival is 'putting No. 1 first' and that the main object of living is to do what you want to do and get as much as you can for yourself irrespective of the harm it may do to others. Since there is no respect for property in their own homes, and they are in and out of any other homes which will receive them, where they are often fed indiscriminately, their notions of personal property may be hazy, and the distinction between borrowing and stealing somewhat unclear; but they are quite certain that what they want at the moment must be theirs, whereas if they do not happen to feel strongly they can be extremely generous also. Their lives and those of their parents, are a social embodiment of the principle of uncertainty.

It must be appreciated that even if these families are poor, they are rejected not because of this, but because they make little or no effort to keep up standards in the face of it. Poverty is something which is still experienced by many in the welfare state, and which any working-class family can fall into suddenly through unemployment, accident or ill health. Patched clean clothes are embarrassing but excusable; unpatched dirty ones are not.

Crime

It is well known that crime rates (the rates per 100,000 population in the relevant age groups) have been rising steadily since World War II, and that they have been accompanied by considerable increases in the prison population, now at a daily average of 32–35,000; three times as much as in the 1920s; and in the numbers in approved schools and other institutions, and on probation. There was a dip in the figures from 1951 to 1954, but since then they have moved upwards steadily. The rates for those convicted of violent crimes and sexual crimes rose even in the period of the downturn and it is only very recently that the curve for sexual crimes has levelled off. It is equally well known that the rates have risen with particular rapidity in the seventeen to twenty-one age group.

There has been a good deal of argument on the linked questions of whether the figures of crimes known to the police adequately represent the actual number of offences committed, and whether the high concentration of crime in the working class is real, or merely a result of differential arrest rates. Recent American studies indicate that there is a reasonably stable relationship between reported and unreported crime. The higher the number of offences actually committed and the more serious they are, the greater the likelihood of arrest and prosecution. The court appearance rate thus very much understates the number of crimes committed but remains representative of the trend. Working-class boys commit offences more often, and are more likely to commit serious offences; the higher rate of working-class crime is therefore valid.[2] Further, the lower the stratum within the working class, the less amenable are offenders to treatment measures. This would accord with the greater degree of commitment to a deviant way of life deriving from the situation as outlined above, and the higher incidence of total or virtual abandonment of children leading not only to homelessness and rootlessness, but also to an inability to form the necessary affectional relationships and live an ordered life.

Persistent crime constitutes a small corner of working-class life, and is largely concentrated in the stratum described above. Adolescent crime, like motoring offences, covers a large area. It is clear from the figures, and from various studies that some form of criminal activity is by no means uncommon, certainly amongst the lower stratum, but that it ceases for the majority in early adulthood. Much of it is associated with the influence of 'ganging' (to be understood in the sense of somewhat inchoate friendship groups, and not highly structured, led groups), and the status competition within these groups. This is not, however, a sufficient explanation by itself.

Attempts at explanation fall roughly into two categories. The first depends on Merton's suggestion that the mass media impose a success ethic to which working-class boys subscribe, but which cannot be achieved because of structural blockages, largely in education; and that this then produces a problem of adaptation which is for the most part met by accepting one's lot, but is solved for a minority through bypassing the blockages by means of crime. This does not explain why the form of adaptation changes for most boys in early adulthood, but it could explain the rapid rise in adolescent crime in practically all industrialised societies since World War II on the grounds that aspirations have risen and cannot be fulfilled: for example, higher reference groups and thus more relative deprivation. Unfortunately, the few reliable studies do not confirm the view that aspirations are more unreasonable among delinquents than non-delinquents, at least in terms of jobs.

The other approach is that the values and norms already discussed as important, must be learned by the adolescent, and that in doing so he exaggerates them; and this brings him in conflict with the law. Physical strength as undue violence; the 'binge' blown up into a search for excitement; autonomy as strong feelings of not caring what anyone says; living for today turned into the unthinking impulse which fails to take account of the consequences and is strongly backed by status competition in the group—these all tend towards a drift into criminality. The break-up of groups on marriage, and the acceptance of responsibility tones down the strength of these traits to the normal working-class level, leaving behind an increased number who are predisposed, because of maladjustment, or a really deviant background, to form the stage army of adult criminals. This approach seems more attractive, but it offers no reason why there should have been such a rapid increase in the postwar period. Has working-class socialisation become so much more difficult so suddenly, and if so why?

Once we move into adult crime, we perceive the emergence of a more professional type of criminal and, to a limited degree, a subculture of crime; but for the most part the habitual criminal is a poor, sad, soul with strong psychiatric disabilities, and often extremely isolated. By far the greatest number of crimes are comparatively minor ones, and this is true of the habitual criminal also. Similarly, the majority of cases are tried in magistrates' courts and the most common sentence is a fine; the practice of fining is also increasing in the higher courts. In general, the pattern of crime and punishment tends to fall into four groups: the first offenders who have higher success rates whatever their age or crime; those who are sent to prison for the first time who equally have very high success rates whatever their age or crime; those who commit a few offences and often get increasingly heavy sentences, and then stop; and the real recidivists who increasingly turn into a stage army as one moves along the age groups. The majority fall into the first three groups. Most criminal careers are comparatively short, and in each age group there is a new recruitment, but a fallout from each group continues to commit offences.

Thus, for the most part, the offending population consists of working-class men, particularly from the lower strata; and progressively the more normal tend to be weeded out, leaving a collection of the extremely deviant, most of whom would in any case have become downwardly mobile, but who are often helped to do so by repeated institutionalisation.[3]

A somewhat different problem is the very large number of motoring offenders, most of whom are not in any real sense criminals. If there is a 'typical' offence of the 1960s it is the motoring offence and the proportion of middle-class people is, of course, much higher. Nevertheless Willett shows that those guilty of repeated serious traffic offences have often committed other types of offences as well, and belong to the class of persistent offenders.[4]

Drugs and alcohol

It is not proposed to say much here about drug addiction, which affects a very small part of the population, largely the deviant fringe of the young adult section. It is probable that heroin addiction is growing and although it need not have serious consequences, the type of people who become addicts, and the circumstances in which it is taken, tend to make it so. This may also be true of cannabis, which does not lead to physical dependence, and has no serious ill effects if taken in moderation. The danger in these drugs, as in others, is that they are being taken 'for kicks' by sections of the younger population who are likely to be destroyed by lack of foresight in using them. However, in view of the very large number of prescriptions for barbiturates, issued mainly to adults, and the dangers of combining them with other drugs, such as alcohol, these represent a much more serious threat, especially as they can be highly physically addictive. Deaths from barbiturate poisoning are rising and because of the large-scale use of the drug in medicine (heroin has very limited medical uses, and cannabis none), are likely to continue to do so.[5] It is not clear how far drug addiction is a specifically working-class phenomenon in England but it seems likely that the recent growth has been much more concentrated in young working-class people.

By far the most dangerous drug is, of course, alcohol, largely because of its association with road accidents. As car ownership becomes more widely distributed in the working class, the numbers killed and injured from this cause is likely to rise, and young people are bound to be particularly affected. Road safety campaigns and improved roads do, however, seem to be having some success, as the accident rate per vehicle mile does not appear to be rising.[6] There is also an association between drink and assaults. For instance, an investigation into crimes of violence found that they were often committed when drunk, and in the vicinity of pubs.[7]

There is a difference between heavy drinking, which can be controlled, and alcoholic addiction, which cannot. Some estimates put the number of actual addicts very high, but nobody really knows how many there are. The common stereotype of the addict is the middle- or upper-class drunk and Alcoholics Anonymous deals mainly with these. The working-class addict is a much more difficult proposition and there are probably a higher proportion who are untreatable.

Illegitimacy

There are no very comprehensive studies of illegitimacy, but it seems likely that it is highest in the lowest stratum of the working class, although how the other strata compare with the non-manual categories is very difficult to say.[8] It may well be that it is inversely related to the combined effect of the use of contraceptives and the capacity to pay for an abortion. There may also be rather more acceptance of the illegitimate child, even amongst the respectable working class.

There are two major categories of illegitimates, those who are accepted into a family, or who are in reality normal children of a family but the parents are unmarried and cohabiting (often as a result of restrictive divorce laws); and those situations where the mother is already, or becomes cut off from her family. The Newcastle on Tyne study[9], confirmed by others, indicates that the large majority of illegitimates are of the former type. Some 40 per cent of illegitimate maternities in this group were born to couples who were cohabiting in what appeared to be stable unions. Cohabitation is spread through all classes, but is probably higher in the lower working class. The proportion of less stable cohabitation is unknown, but it is probably common amongst deviants. Here, however, the culture of the stratum is probably of much greater importance in its effect on the child than the fact of illegitimacy.

About a quarter of the illegitimacies are in single women who are not cohabiting, and these form the main problem, but in a considerable number of cases the mother and child are accepted by the girl's family, and this provides a stable family background, although not as near the normal family as the stable cohabitations. The most difficult group, and the Newcastle study suggests that the proportion may be as low as 4 per cent, is those who are totally unsupported.

All illegitimates are at risk in both physical and mental health. Further information on illegitimacy is likely to emerge from a large-scale study of poverty among fatherless families which is now in progress.

Marriage breakdown

Although compared with the national figures, families with heads in the non-manual grades go to Marriage Guidance Bureaus twice as often as might be expected, it remains true that in 1952–54 about half of those counselled were in the manual grades, and some 70 per cent had an elementary education only (before the 1944 Education Act). Manual workers more often come with problems relating to housing, low incomes and ill health, but where personal defects were cited, these were more often selfishness, temper, drinking and gambling; whereas non-manual couples more often came with sexual problems and those related to immaturity in husband and wife (the differences are not, however, very great).[10]

It is not very easy to link these figures up with the information on separation and divorce. We do not know the variations between classes in those apparently helped, and in any case neither the marriage counselling data, nor the data on separation and divorce are sufficiently full to allow comparison. It can only be recorded that separation and divorce have been increasing over the marriage cohorts. A recent study shows that at the tenth anniversary, the proportion of all marriages divorced increased from 1 per cent in the 1930–34 cohort to 5 per cent in the 1940–44 cohort. This was probably an effect of the war, and the fifth anniversary figures for post-war cohorts are declining. Perhaps those marriages which survived the war are more stable; but it is not clear how far postwar tendencies to earlier marriage may affect the position in the long term.

In general, the marriages most likely to end in separation and divorce are the small number of those without children where the bride was under twenty, but there are too few of these to affect the figures very much. More common are the situations where the bride was under twenty, and there are children, particularly when she was pregnant at marriage. Since the trend towards younger marriage increases as one moves down the occupational strata and the illegitimacy rate probably also shows this trend, it seems likely that the working class contributes greatly to these figures and the numbers of breakdowns will probably increase, although whether this is greater than the increase in the population at risk is not as yet apparent. There may also have been other changes in the situation since 1951, when the survey from which the above information is derived was carried out.[11] It does not cover remarriage; the remarriage rate, which is affected by the actual number of divorces, is rising with the divorce rate, particularly, of course, in the under thirties.[12] Divorce does not affect the working class in anything like the same degree as does separation, the figures for which show similar trends to divorce.

Reference was made above to figures from the 1951 study. Margaret Wynn[13] estimates from various sources that in the early 1960s there were about 250,000 women separated from their husbands and they had some 375,000 children. We know very little indeed about these families in general but the recent poverty survey confirms Wynn's contention that they often have very low incomes. Of 280,000 families with two or more children whose resources were below national assistance levels, 75,000 with 205,000 children were fatherless. Since many fatherless families including most unmarried mothers and many separated mothers have only one child, this considerably understates the extent of poverty in this group.

Widowhood is, of course, a very different kind of family breakdown, but nevertheless the loss of a father often has serious effects, particularly where there are young children and the mother is unable to work. Declining male mortality is reducing the numbers of young widows and their remarriage rate is rising, but the increased longevity of older women, and the higher marriage rate is likely to increase the number of pensioner widows.[14]

The consequences of marriage breakdown

Although our information regarding deprived children is very limited, a few things can be said. In the first place, the studies quoted above show that there are fewer children in families who obtain divorces, than those who do not; but this is accounted for by the higher number of those who divorce at short marriage duration. Children's Department statistics show a steady increase in long-term cases coming from separated or divorced families, and thus an increasing number of older children, with parents still in the background who have been subjected to considerable periods of strain. No doubt the increasing popularity of marriage and the increase in numbers in their first ten years of marriage explains much of this, and no attempt has yet been made to relate numbers and types of children coming into care with the numbers at risk. Nevertheless, from the point of view of those who have to deal with them, the difficulty of the problem has very much increased.

There is no useful information about class differences, but it is probable that the great majority of the cases come from the lower section of the working class (and, very sensibly, over 70 per cent of all foster mothers are working-class).[15] Deviant families contribute out of all proportion, and although their children are less often seriously disturbed, they may well be of dull intelligence and unsocialised. Since death has ceased to be a major factor in the removal of parents, there are fewer orphans, or children one of whose parents has died; and this makes the proportion of disturbed cases loom even larger, even though the proportion of the population in the relevant age group in the care of local authority Children's Departments remains stable at about 5 per 1,000.[16]

Margaret Wynn[17] estimates that in the early 1960s, there were 260,000 children living with widowed mothers; 80,000 with divorced mothers; 375,000 with separated mothers, and 70,000 with unmarried mothers, making 785,000 in all. There may be some overlap with the numbers in short term and even long term care, but it is probably permissible to add on the latter, and even this does not include those in long term care in voluntary institutions. Many of those living with their mothers are not in any sense deprived, but many are subject to considerable pressures which may result in disturbed personalities and deviant behaviour. We would expect the majority of them to be working-class, simply because manual workers represent some two-thirds of the population, and children of manual workers a higher proportion of the child population. It is, however, true that they come disproportionately from the lower and deviant strata and thus represent a special problem in support, protection and rehabilitation.

The future of the working class

It is now time to try to draw together the threads of the various trends in working-class life discussed in previous chapters. In doing so it is assumed that the Government continues to manage the economy with at least enough success to avoid the worst consequences of its export and balance of payment problems; and that the United States also manages to avoid a prolonged slump. Furthermore, it is assumed that if Britain eventually gets into the Common Market, we will manage to avoid the worst of the economic consequences; so that while there may be considerable problems of redeployment of labour, there will be no continuing widespread unemployment.

In the next ten years (up to the mid 1970s) the labour force is likely to be fairly static, although the population is slowly rising. The actual numbers depend a good deal upon immigration control. It is not expected that entry into the Common Market would produce much of a flow from the continent, and the main question is the level of inflow allowed from the Commonwealth. An influx of single, adaptable, trainable workers from this source would be a godsend to British industry, but large numbers of single men produce considerable social problems, and men with families very much add to the dependency rate. Culture clash, colour and housing shortages also complicate the issue; and the net effect is likely to be continuing restriction.

The working population will not rise as fast as the non-working population, and is being cut into by rapid increases in those in further education to which will be added (if it takes place) the increase in the school leaving age by one year in 1970. It will not be until after 1975 that the low birth rate in the prewar period and the high birth rate subsequently will begin to swing the balance the other way. Advances in medicine are likely to reduce mortality in children and to prolong the lives of old people and the disabled, but whether they can cut the sickness rate among the working population sufficiently to offset these extra burdens is doubtful.

The main reason for the slight increase in the labour force is likely to be the continued rise in the employment of married women in the thirty-five to fifty age group. This is already an important factor in working-class life, where the trend to early marriage and earlier completion of the family has been strongest. Presumably industry will demonstrate a growing adaptation to the needs of married women, and there will be some growth in training and retraining. It is likely, however, that women will continue to contribute primarily to unskilled and semiskilled manufacturing industry and to service occupations, and that the part-time element will be high.[1]

If we add to this the very great likelihood that the efficient use of contraception will become usual except possibly in parts of the lower strata, and the considerable possibility that Roman Catholics will be allowed also to take part in this, considerable changes for the family are likely. Fertility rates of Roman Catholic immigrant and other lower strata women may well fall and the mean ultimate family size may therefore not increase quite so much as expected, but it is difficult to say whether the probably opposite effects of expectation of a double income for a considerable part of the working life and the increased efficiency of contraception, have yet had their major effects on fertility.

It seems likely that the trend towards reduction in unskilled work and the expansion of the skilled sector will continue. Assuming that retraining and transfer of labour keeps up with the, rather slow, rate of investment and technological change, there should be a considerable increase in mobility in the working class. Any increase in the efficiency of the educational system in awarding merit will increase both the rate of upward and downward mobility.

Geographical mobility is likely to rise steadily. One of the major problems has been the peculiarities of the housing market, since the

9

rapidly increasing local authority sector has restrictive rules requiring previous residence in the area of the authority for varying periods. The rising tide of double incomes will almost certainly lead to more home ownership, and there is already a trend towards the sale of local authority houses. The balance between the cost of mortgages, and other expenses of owner occupation, and local authority rent is at present very much in favour of the latter (about 20 per cent of income as against 9 per cent), but there is strong pressure to match local authority rents with the rise in incomes and an increasing proportion are likely to find the differences much smaller. However, the low rent local authority house is likely to remain attractive in the years of family formation when there is only one income. Since the restrictive force of mortgages on mobility rises rapidly in the forties, when the period of the mortgage begins to contract, a good deal depends upon the pressure to move in double income families in their thirties.

It is, however, likely that kinship pressures combined with rising car ownership (at about 8 per cent for the whole population) will cause a fanning out round urban centres rather than long distance moves, and this is already happening; especially where, as in the larger urban centres, relocation within industry is possible in the same area.

In education, the expectation would be that the proportion of those who are at least prepared to provide a background of reasonable affection and support and allow the school to do the rest, will rise steadily; and reduced pressure on income is likely to make it easier for families to bear with longer periods of higher education. Since the general skill content will be upward, the likelihood is that there will be more encouragement for further education, but whether this would apply to the standards and outlook needed for university education is more problematical. Since, however, the shortage of university places and facilities is likely to continue, the level of applications will probably continue to run at a higher level than can be accepted for a long time to come—although limited aspiration to science and technology may well continue to keep places empty in these fields.

Theoretical approaches

Having now outlined the background, we can turn to further discussion of the approach to analysis which was briefly set out in the opening chapter. It was there suggested that acceptance of inferior status was dependent upon a number of factors, those specifically mentioned being: power, helplessness, restricted referents, selective rationalisation, feelings of limited worth and acculturation processes in general. Of these, power, helplessness, and feelings of limited worth are structural factors which are not likely to alter in the short run and, for brevity's sake, we do not discuss them further. We do not have space for more than a brief look at the others, and do no more than to suggest some lines of thought.

1. Referents[2]

(a) *Historical referents*. Some of the most important referent areas are historical in the sense of relating one's present situation to what has happened in the immediate past. Having done better or worse than one's parents is often a standard of reference and it can be both individual and in terms of reference groups. Where intergenerational mobility is high, the comparisons are sharpened both in terms of relative advantage and relative deprivation. Where the general trend in incomes and living standards is upward, the normal situation is relative advantage, and downward mobility and deprivation thus becomes more of a problem to which adjustment is necessary. It is obvious that this is very much the present situation in the working class.

(b) *Membership referents*. As has been pointed out, many of the comparisons made are of status within the groups to which the individual belongs. If he is a skilled worker is he better or worse off than other skilled workers; is he keeping up with other men in his workshop; is she a better housewife than her friends? The force of these comparisons often depends upon the range of these groups, and the degree to which one is closely associated with the other members. The degree to which there may be changes of this kind is very difficult to estimate, but in a work situation which is liable to considerable change due to technological innovation the worker may well find himself increasingly likely to make such comparisons. Equally, increases in comparability as a consumer (the object of much advertising) may affect the housewife with money to spend.

(*c*) *Comparative referents*. The most obvious type of comparison is with groups outside those of which one is a member. The strong tendency is for these comparisons to be restricted to groups to which one might possibly have access; more distant comparisons moving progressively into the field of fantasy and thus acting as compensatory individual mechanisms, or demonstrating a degree of maladjustment. A relatively high mobility potential is liable to increase this type of comparison. Formal differences in status, for example, in skill status, and the need for a qualification of some kind enhances the differentiation between groups. The blurring of differentiation over a large part of the working class reduces the likelihood of clear comparisons of this kind, but the increasing emphasis upon educational levels over a wide area tends to reintroduce them; and the association of skill with training and with restrictive entry tends to mark off the more skilled manual worker. Thus, the move towards higher educational levels and skills increases the degree of definition of reference groups and thus the likelihood of thinking in terms of comparative referents.

2. *Selective rationalisation*

The actual choice of referents obviously affects the way in which the process of selective rationalisation works. One may see oneself at the top, in the middle or at the bottom. The nearer one gets to the bottom of any scale the more likely it is that the actual referent will either be a group which is in some special sense worse off ('At least we've got a roof over our heads'); or explains away personal deviance, such as the value of alcohol ('A little nip does you good'), or of autonomy ('I don't care for no one; I do what I like'), or of pleasure in general. The important point here is that the major value is not necessarily sociological, but may be psychological; the maintenance of that indefinable but supremely important feeling of self-respect and worth. It is more often maintained by some mechanism coming within the sphere of interrelationships, and indicating that one is wanted, or at least accepted, but it can also be maintained in considerable isolation.

3. *Acculturation*

The acculturation process covers, amongst other things, the way that referents and rationalisations are conveyed to children and thus maintained in the next generation. The characteristic of the post-World War II generation is that considerable changes have taken place within which it is necessary to find a legitimate set of role relationships, and the parental problem of acculturation has thus become much more difficult. In this way a much heavier burden is thrown on to the adolescent and young adult, in that he has more often to explore roles, referents and rationalisations himself. The school may or may not help him in this task. For the most part he succeeds in solving these problems; sometimes he does not. The exploration gives rise to a colourful fringe of beatniks, hippies and other oddities; and to higher levels of temporary and perhaps more permanent breakdown, in terms of crime or drug taking; and in some of these cases to serious unintended consequences upon others —the victims of crime, the illegitimate children. For the most part, however, the problem is solved by an adaptation of the basic way of life of parents, or by upward mobility and the acceptance of a different way of life.

There is, of course, another field of acculturation; where people are moved, usually by slum clearance, from a known to an unknown community. It is obvious from the Dagenham study that the cultural shock involved can be overcome, but it may take a generation to do it.

Density of relationships

It was also suggested in the first chapter that an important sphere of study was in the number and quality of contacts with others. There is no space here to go into this in detail, but the sense of community derives not only from proximity to kin, and to a feeling that everyone is in the same boat, but also to what Frankenburg calls *redundancy*, the additional complexities of interrelationships which arise from continually seeing people in multiple roles. Multiple role relationships, however, are more common in Ambridge than in Coronation Street, despite the attempt in the latter programme to produce them. The traditional working class as it was resembled Ambridge more closely, though it tended to lack the settled relationships with middle-class people living in the community who provided leadership and added to the variety of organisations: the schoolmaster, the squire, the vicar. It is probable that the traditional situation still exists in more isolated, and single industry, communities, where working-class leadership is itself stronger. It is doubtful how far it exists elsewhere.

A distinction was made between close contacts and general contacts and this is relevant to the traditional working-class situation where strong ties with kin living nearby were much more the rule for the women, the children, and reluctantly, the men, who were more concerned with friendship ties. Outside this much of the contact was not in terms of multiple roles but was a much more superficial acquaintanceship sometimes expressed as neighbouring; supportive to the degree to which one gets used to the familiar, and oppressive to the extent that one is forced to meet continually a lot of people one doesn't like. Privacy in its real sense of 'keeping yourself to yourself' *when you want to*, was always an extremely strong value in traditional working-class life, but difficult to maintain. It is to a considerable extent from this that the tradition of not going into other people's houses unless invited arises. It is thus possible to shed general contacts with some sense of relief, whereas close contacts cannot easily be shed, and lead to deprivation if broken.

The upper and middle strata

It is now possible to consider what is happening to different parts of the working class in more detail. In doing so, three methods of cutting up the working-class cake will be discussed together. The first is the division by strata—upper, middle, lower, deviant—and I propose to consider here the upper and middle together, then the lower and the deviant strata. Secondly, there is an age split which consists roughly of those who were born before 1935–40 and subsequently: those who for the most part have no real experience of widespread poverty and unemployment in a society which was both helpless and uncommitted to managing its affairs for the benefit of the major part of its people (however inefficiently); and those who have been adolescent and then married under the newer dispensation. Thirdly, there is the difference between life seen from a male and a female point of view.

We start with a brief discussion of affluence and *embourgeoisement*. In what has now become a much quoted article,[3] Goldthorpe and Lockwood argued that affluence was not really leading to the working class becoming middle-class, but rather that various aspects of change in the middle and working classes were leading to a convergence in which the use of collective action (e.g. trade unionism, political parties) was for the working class becoming merely a means to attain individual and family ends, as against feelings of collective solidarity; and the middle classes were more often using trade unionism for the same purpose and relaxing their previous strongly individualist tenets. Thus the emphasis in both tended to be upon family centredness. The changes did not necessarily mean that the worker crossed the dividing line and became middle-class, since he might well retain his working-class normative identification and merely retreat from feelings of solidarity with the working class; thus becoming a 'privatised' worker.

This analysis is useful in that it points to a situation where changes in some parts of the worker's behaviour and goals has taken place which bring him nearer to middle-class behaviour, while he remains in other important respects much more like the traditional worker. In a preliminary report on their Luton study[4] the same authors comment upon differences between 229 manual workers and 54 lower-level white-collar workers. Although they were very similar in income, possessions and house ownership, the manual workers were much less interested in the work itself, doing it only for the money, and saw much less chance of promotion. The manual workers also seemed to indulge in rather less entertaining of people, other than kin, than the non-manual workers, though the evidence here is very much affected by the fact that far more manual workers lacked local roots, and must be regarded, pending further analysis, as uncertain. The working men and their wives made little attempt to join middle-class organisations and stuck to those entirely working-class in membership; furthermore they continued to vote Labour by a large majority.

While Goldthorpe and Lockwood may well be right in claiming that the privatised worker exists, it seems unlikely that their study will throw much light upon how far this is a new phenomenon, or whether it is related primarily to affluence. The highly mobile worker looking for money and prepared to give up the supposed advantages of the traditional working-class community must surely have always existed. Deliberately taking a sample of geographically highly mobile workers may well have produced an uncharacteristic minority, since most workers do not move considerable distances and it does not follow, if it is established that such displaced workers have many working-class characteristics, that they are a 'crucial case' proving the existence of a substantial proportion of a continuum of which this is an extreme. Their very displacement and isolation may in fact make it very difficult for them to shed working-class characteristics. A much more crucial comparison is of working-class people settled for some time by choice in middle-class estates not too far away from kin, and the Woodford study contributes some information about this. The study shows that the Woodford manual workers tend to fall midway between their Bethnal Green counterparts and the Woodford middle class; but more resemble the middle class when they think of themselves as belonging to it. Thus the manual worker family head who describes himself as 'middle-class' more often owns his own house, has a car and a telephone, goes to church and belongs to clubs. Unfortunately, Willmott and Young have not pursued at length on their large sample the complex effects of length of residence, different family compositions, presence or absence nearby of close relations, and age differences. It may well be that their large sample was too generally defined to encompass complex breakdowns, since extracting families of particular compositions and ages very much reduces the numbers. Further research ought to concentrate much more upon specific subgroups, covering various combinations of the major factors as indicated above.

What all this seems to indicate is that most real upward mobility is based upon education or, for women, marrying upwards; that there may be a limited number who do, perhaps early in life, become indistinguishable from the lower middle class, but for the most part, affluence is used to buy things and has only a limited effect upon the accepted patterns of living once these are established. How far there may be a difference between the younger and older generation is not clear, but it would probably take several generations to produce patterns of family living which were indistinguishable from the lower middle class.

Even if this happened, there would still be considerable differences in the work situation in terms both of work content and promotion prospects. Goldthorpe and Lockwood are not convincing on the question of job satisfaction (which they find is less among the manual than non-manual workers) because of the special nature of their sample. A study of job satisfaction made on a large sample by Wilensky[5] in America found that social class was not as important a prediction of work alienation as work situations which put the worker under pressure both from the job flow and from the supervisory hierarchy; frustration in one's career; strong family pressures stemming from large numbers of children and shortage of saving. The Wilensky sample seems to be very deficient in lower working-class respondents but the thirty-five included show distinctly higher work alienation than the rest, while no difference is shown in the middle ranges. Since most skilled manual workers are at the top of their tree, and most junior white-collar workers at the bottom, it is difficult to believe that lack of interest in the job is more prevalent in the former.

The lower stratum

While more attention has been paid by sociologists to affluence and *embourgeoisement* it is likely that the most important effect of affluence is upon the lower stratum. Since some of the most important referents are historical, those who are better off than their parents and especially if they are increasingly acquiring possessions and not losing work status, are likely to be well content. They are not likely to be much concerned even if Titmuss, rather than Lydall or Kaldor, is right and there has in fact been little real change in the distribution of income and wealth over the whole population.

Those, however, who are not doing better than their parents have to face condemnation both from their historical and comparative referents; and where, as seems likely, the majority of the working class is pulling away from a minority who remain in poverty, the frustrations experienced by this minority must be considerable, and must be difficult to offset by selective rationalisation.

Furthermore, the lower stratum is being slowly infiltrated by coloured immigrants. What proportion they are of this stratum is difficult to say, but it is probably increasing in relation to the native English, or Irish, as the general level of jobs given to white workers rises. The immigrants suffer from problems of discrimination, and this introduces another discontented element in the lower stratum.

We do not have enough information at present to put any reasonably reliable figures to the above statements. In a survey carried out in 1959 in the United States,[6] about one-fifth (10·4 m) of all U.S. families were defined as poor after very careful investigation of income. Of these 73 per cent had worked in 1959 but their actual earnings fell far short of what they might have earned, and their gross disposable income was very much lower than the poverty line adopted. Data about past earnings show chronic low earnings over long periods, and in the United States this means very limited health insurance and pension rights. If we consider the occupations of the fathers of the heads of poor families and then of the heads, we find that of the unskilled and farm workers 65 per cent stayed in the same category, 23 per cent became skilled or semiskilled and 12 per cent white-collar workers. In the skilled and semiskilled category 41 per cent stayed the same, 49 per cent went down and 10 per cent up; and of the white-collar workers 40 per cent remained white-collar, 28 per cent became skilled or semiskilled, and 32 per cent unskilled or farm workers. Of the 630 fathers of heads, 456 were unskilled; and 369 of the sons were unskilled. Since lack of skill over this period has become substantially more serious the 369 sons have become more restricted in their life chances, and thus liable to unfavourable historical and comparative referents.

Thus the lower stratum is suffering from a number of increasingly severe pressures:

1. *Upward mobility* of those who, despite the deficiencies of the educational system, and the anti-academic nature of the culture, manage to use the system to get into higher education. Most of the movements upward are, however, only to better manual jobs and are probably not seriously disruptive.

2. *Downward mobility* of those who, for various reasons, have failed to cope, for example, fatherless families, the mentally ill and subnormal and their families.

3. *Pressure on family links* due to rehousing, which is a proportionately greater financial burden, and thus much more likely to lead to strain and isolation; and also due to the changed position of teenagers.

4. *Culture clash* due to increases in the number of immigrant families, since the main burden of accommodation and assimilation usually falls on the lower stratum.

5. *Poverty*, which is still widespread and may be increasing, and which is much more of a threat to self-respect in a society priding itself on its affluence.

6. *Deviance*, which represents both an actual threat since most of crime is committed in lower class areas, and a potential threat in that the respectable want to prevent their children from falling into it.

All these have existed in varying degrees for some time, and there is no space here to go into detail about the way in which these pressures are changing. It does, however, seem almost certain that, despite the softening effects of selective rationalisation, relative deprivation is increasing in the lower stratum, and is being accompanied by a weakening in the density of relationships. The vertical schisms in the lower stratum, caused by the existence of communities alien to each other, including the scattered clusters of deviants, are intensifying; and the subtle effects of rehousing policies are tending both to cut up the extended family, and to remove many of the more respectable elements in the older communities. The young/old split in the lower stratum is seriously affected by these stresses, which fall heavily upon the adolescent and upon the young marrieds with children. The adolescents find it more difficult to struggle upwards into maturity, the young marrieds to avoid poverty and the adverse effect of the somewhat disorganised society in which they live.

The personalisation of women has had less impact in the lower stratum, where there is least capacity for handling relationships. The social worker's belief that every family ought to have a set of understandings as complex as the middle-class or upper working-class family, is least appropriate in this stratum—which is the one in which she usually works. Yet personalisation is spreading downwards and traditional role separations are weakening. We shall, however, for a long time yet have with us the overworked, exploited and poverty-stricken wife, anxious only to serve a husband who has been brought up to expect her to act this role, and who plays his part accordingly.

The danger which Michael Young foresaw in *The Rise of the Meritocracy* is not yet with us; but in a world in which the enhancement of personalisation by the use of what Bernstein[7] describes as 'elaborated codes' of speech, those who are least capable of sweetening relationships and avoiding conflict are liable to be increasingly rejected. The lower stratum, as one end of the distribution, is likely to appear as deviant simply because of this; in so far as it is heavily weighted with those who have gravitated there because of extreme incapacity, and contains many people from alien cultures not yet even accommodated, let alone assimilated, and suffering from the visibility of colour, it is likely increasingly to become a rejected minority.

The Deviants

As noted previously, although the deviants are largely concentrated in the lower stratum, they form a wedge the point of which reaches up into other reaches of the working class. They might be classified as follows:

1. *The unsocialised* described in some detail in the Radby study, and books on problem families. They represent patches of a form of subculture but, since the basis of their lack of socialisation is extreme individualism, they can hardly be described in group terms. Some are families, others have become detached and isolated, sometimes through institutionalisation, and have lost the ability to earn, to plan, or to form relationships.

2. *The psychopathic.* These overlap with the unsocialised and might be described as having the same characteristics in a form so extreme as to make it a recognisable syndrome.

3. *The professionals.* The comparatively normal section of the deviant population, who lead asocial lives because they like living that way. The community of prostitutes is very much of this type; and there is a degree of group feeling amongst a number of professional criminals in the larger towns.

4. *The addicted.* The small coterie of drug addicts, and the much larger collection of working-class drunks (who are quite different from the middle-class drunk and much more difficult to deal with).

5. *The transitional.* This category covers the considerable numbers of the temporarily deviant, of whom the major contingent are the working-class adolescents who fall foul of the law, but are not committed to a criminal career. There are, however, a number of others who are going through phases where they may be temporarily antisocial.

In general it will be seen that these people can be reclassified into four groups: the unsocialised individualist, whose progress is well described in Klein's opening chapters; the deviant subcultures such as the prostitutes; the psychiatric cases, mainly of the type psychiatrists do not know how to cure; and those who have broken down under the pressure of circumstances and will be all right when these circumstances are removed, but may shift into the psychiatric category if they are not.

It cannot be overemphasised that most of these people are of working-class culture, particularly in their own versions of the aims and values and the family relationships which obtain in the traditional working class. Nevertheless, they do not for the most part constitute a subculture in any real sense: they are too absorbed with themselves and their own problems, and too individualistic to do so. They form an inchoate collection, who only have in common the fact that they are rejected by most of the working class, and by society in general.

The stretching process in the working class

Thus, it would appear that the working class is, in a number of ways, undergoing a stretching process. The upper stratum while retaining its own identity is taking on many of the characteristics of the middle class; there is a general stretching of family ties and a lowering of the density of family relationships, partly as a result of increasing geographical mobility, partly due to vertical mobility, and partly to rehousing policies; there is an increasing gap between the older and younger generations, since the adolescents and the young marrieds are living under radically altered conditions; there is an increasing gap between the poor and the well off; and there is a new series of immigrant communities.

If the stretching process is leading to some cracking at the seams, and to an increased number of those unable to stand up to it, for the most part the structure is holding together extremely well and showing great adaptability. Nevertheless, the strain is bound to tell, and it is being felt strongly in the working class. Professor Titmuss, whose work and ideas have revolutionised public thinking upon the welfare state, spoke only too wisely when he said in his Inaugural Lecture in September 1951:

The outlook on life of those groups with no incremental ladder in front of them, no middle-class ethos of economic ascent, no provision of lump sum payments at sixty and more worth-while pensions in old age, must be difficult for other groups, differently placed, to comprehend. Comparisons are inevitable in a society which has promised and tried hard to practice social justice, fair shares and equal educational opportunities. To the extent that social benefits get out of harmony and are felt to be out of harmony with the cycle of actual and desired needs, the greater the likelihood of social and psychological stress.

In these situations, the family seeks a new equilibrium. Somehow or other it has to conform to the contrary pulls of a changing society. We know little, however, of the forces that are shaping the norms of family life. We do not understand the fundamental reasons for the falling birth rate; for the greater popularity of marriage, for the rising esteem of children in our society, or the significance of the large increase in the number of married women who now leave their homes to work in factory and office. On the surface, there are contradictions here, just as there are when the problem of incentives, perhaps the crucial problem in economic inquiry today, is considered alongside these trends. Maybe there is in process a new division of labour in the family, a rearrangement of role, of function; a new calculus of effort and reward in which the frontier between workplace and home is becoming blurred. Such processes, which may upset current theories about industrial productivity, may also lead to situations of stress in the home and the factory; new situations of dishonesty in which men find their inherited system of norms no longer rewarding. But while families may be hurt by these stresses, people rarely die from them. The maladjustments in society do not now kill as they did in the nineteenth century. Medical science at least keeps people alive. Our old indices of social disorder are now less useful. We cannot so easily measure the complex sicknesses of a complex society; the prevalence of the stress diseases of modern civilization, the instabilities of family relationships or the extent of mental ill-health in the community. Difficulties of accurate measurement should not prevent us, however, from seeking to extend our knowledge of the causes at work.[8]

References and further reading

References cited in chapter 1 are not repeated for individual chapters

CHAPTER 2

1. K. Davis, *Human Society*, Macmillan, 1949; K. Davis and W. E. Moore, 'Some principles of stratification', *Am. Sociol. Rev.* 10 (1945), 242–9.

2. C. Wright Mills, *The Power Élite*, O.U.P. 1956.

3. S. Ossowski, *Class Structure in the Social Consciousness*, Routledge, 1963.

4. M. Young, *The Rise of the Meritocracy*, Thames and Hudson, 1958; Penguin.

5. R. Frankenberg, *Communities in Britain*, Penguin, 1966.

6. D. Lockwood, 'Sources of variation in working class images of society', *Sociol. Rev.* 14 (1966), 249–68.

7. J. H. Goldthorpe and D. Lockwood, 'Affluence and the British class structure', *Sociol. Rev.* 11 (1963), 133–63.

8. W. L. Warner, M. Meeker and K. Eells, *Social Class in America*, Science Research Associates, 1949.

9. A. F. Davis, 'Prestige of occupations', *Brit. J. Sociol.* 3 (1952), 134–47.

10. A. Inkeles and P. H. Rossi, 'National comparisons of occupational prestige', *Am. J. Sociol.* 6 (1956), 329–39.

11. M. Young and P. Willmott, 'Social grading by manual workers', *Brit. J. Sociol.* 7 (1956), 337–45.

12. For the methods used see Registrar-General, *Classification of Occupations*, 1960.

13. S. M. Lipset and R. Bendix, *Social Mobility in Industrial Society*, University of California Press, 1966.

14. D. Lockwood, *The Blackcoated Worker*, Unwin, 1958.

15. G. Routh, *Occupation and Pay in Great Britain 1906–60*, C.U.P. 1965.

16. W. L. Warner and P. S. Lunt, *The Social Life of a Modern Community*, Yale University Press, 1941.

17. A. Hollingshead, *Elmtown's Youth*, Science Editions, 1961.

18. H. Wilson, *Delinquency and Parental Neglect*, Allen & Unwin, 1962.

CHAPTER 3

1. W. Baldamus, *Efficiency and Effort*, Tavistock, 1961.

2. F. J. Roethlisberger and W. J. Dickson, *Management and the Worker*, Harvard, 1947.

3. M. P. Fogarty, *Personality and Group Relations in Industry*, Longmans, 1956; D. C. Miller and W. H. Form, *Industrial Sociology*, 2nd edn., Harper, 1964. Fogarty contains more British material.

4. W. F. Whyte, *Human Relations in the Restaurant Industry*, McGraw-Hill, 1948.

5. S. Patterson, *Dark Strangers*, Tavistock, 1962 (abridged edition in Penguin, 1965).

6. 'Forecasts of the working population 1966–81', *Ministry of Labour Gazette*, Nov. 1966, pp. 718–21; V. Klein, *Britain's Married Women Workers*, Routledge, 1965.

7. Household Composition, Table 12, *Census*, 1961.

8. H. A. Turner, *Trade Union Growth, Structure and Policy*, Allen & Unwin, 1962.

9. J. H. Goldthorpe and D. Lockwood, 'Affluence and the British class structure', *Sociol. Rev.* 11 (1963), 133–63.

CHAPTER 4

Income
1. G. Routh, *Occupation and Pay in Great Britain 1906–60*, C.U.P., 1965.

2. Unless otherwise stated the Ministry of Labour figures are taken from the current issues of *Statistics on Incomes, Prices, Employment and Production*.

3. H. Lydall, *British Incomes and Savings*, O.U.P. 1955, and *J. Roy. Stat. Soc.* **122** (1959), 33–5; F. W. Paish, *Lloyds Bank Review*, **43** (1957), 1–16.

4. R. Titmuss, *Income Distribution and Social Change*, Allen & Unwin, 1962. See also J. C. Nicholson, *The Redistribution of Income in the U.K. 1959, 1957 and 1953*, Bowes, 1964.

5. S. M. Miller and M. Rein, Poverty, Inequality and Social Policy, in H. S. Becker, ed., *Social Problems: A Modern Approach*, Wiley, 1966. This is by far the best summary of the poverty situation in the U.S.

6. A. R. Prest and T. Stark, *The Manchester School*, **35** (Sept. 1967), 217–44.

7. B. Abel-Smith and P. Townsend, *The Poor and the Poorest*, Occasional Papers in Social Administration, No. 17, 1965.

8. Ministry of Social Security, *Circumstances of Families*, H.M.S.O. 1967.

Education
9. Central Advisory Council for Education—England. *15 to 18*, vols. I and II, H.M.S.O. 1959 (Crowther); *Half our Future*, H.M.S.O. 1963 (Newsom); *Children and Their Primary Schools*, vols. I and II, H.M.S.O. 1967 (Plowden); Committee on Higher Education, *Report* and *Appendix I*, H.M.S.O. 1963 (Robbins); J. W. B. Douglas, *The Home and the School*, MacGibbon & Kee, 1964 (Panther, 1967); J. E. Floud, A. H. Halsey and F. M. Martin, *Social Class and Educational Opportunity*, Heinemann, 1957; P. W. Musgrave, *The Sociology of Education*, Methuen, 1965, Part I.

10. M. Deutsch, *The Influence of Early Social Environment on School Adaptation*, 1963.

11. B. Jackson and D. Marsden, *Education and the Working Class*, Routledge, 1963; Penguin.

12. C. Lacey, 'Some sociological concomitants of academic streaming in a grammar school', *Brit. J. Sociol.* 17 (1966), 245–62; D. H. Hargreaves, *Social Relations in a Secondary School*, Routledge, 1967.

Health: Physical
13. M. Susser and W. Watson, *Sociology in Medicine*, O.U.P. 1962.

14. A. G. Ogilvie and D. J. Newell, *Chronic Bronchitis in Newcastle-on-Tyne*, Livingstone, 1957.

15. J. N. Morris and J. A. Neady, 'Mortality in relation to the father's occupation 1911–50', *Lancet*, 1955, p. 554.

16. P. Stocks, *Annual Report of the British Empire Cancer Campaign 1957 Supplement Pt II*.

17. W. P. D. Logan, *Morbidity Statistics from General Practice*, vol. II *Occupation*, General Register Office Studies on Medical and Population Subjects, No. 14, 1960.

18. A. Cartwright, *Human Relations and Hospital Care*, Routledge, 1964.

19. T. Ferguson and A. N. MacPhail, *Hospital and Community*, O.U.P. 1954; Nuffield Provincial Hospital Trust, *Further Studies in Hospital and Community*, O.U.P. 1962.

Health: Mental illness
20. E. H. Hare, 'The distribution of mental illness in a community' in D. Richter *et al.*, eds, *Aspects of Psychiatric Research*, O.U.P. 1962; J. N. Morris, 'Health and social class', *Lancet*, 1959, pp. 303–5, covers a range of data concerning physical and mental illness; Susser and Watson, *op. cit.*

21. E. M. Goldberg and S. L. Morrison, 'Schizophrenia and social class', *Brit. J. Psychiat.* 109 (1963), 785.

22. Particularly A. B. Hollingshead and F. Redlich, *Social Class and Mental Illness*, Wiley, 1964.

23. R. N. Rapaport, *Community as Doctor*, Tavistock, 1960.

Health: Mental subnormality
24. J. Tizard, *Community Services for the Mentally Handicapped*, O.U.P. 1964; A. M. Clarke and A. D. B. Clarke, *Mental Deficiency—The Changing Outlook*, rev. edn., Methuen, 1965.

25. Z. Stein and M. W. Susser, 'Mental retardation: a cultural syndrome', *Proc. Lond. Conf. Scient. Stud. Ment. Defic.* 1 (1960), 174–8.

Housing
26. M. Bowley, *Housing and the State 1919–44*, Allen & Unwin, 1945.

27. M. Woolf, *The Housing Survey in England and Wales 1964*, Government Social Survey, 1967.

28. J. Cullingworth, *English Housing Trends*, Occasional Papers on Social Administration, No. 13, 1965.

29. *Housing Statistics* 4, January 1967, p. 48. (Issued quarterly by the Ministry of Housing and Local Government.)

30. Ministry of Housing and Local Government, *Our Older Houses*, H.M.S.O. 1966.

31. D. V. Donnison, *The Government of Housing*, Pelican, 1967. By far the best book on housing.

CHAPTER 5

1. Political and Economic Planning, *Family Needs and the Social Services*, P.E.P. and Allen & Unwin, 1961.

CHAPTER 6

1. Registrar General's Quarterly Return for England and Wales, No. 473 1st Quarter (ending 31 March) 1967, H.M.S.O.

2. M. Schofield, *The Sexual Behaviour of Young People*, Longmans, 1965. This study is referred to more fully in chapter 7.

3. E. Bott, *Family and Social Network*, Tavistock, 1957.

4. J. H. Goldthorpe, D. Lockwood, F. Bechhofer and D. Platt, 'The affluent worker and the thesis of embourgeoisement: some preliminary research findings', *Sociology*, 1 (1967), 11–31.

5. R. M. Pierce and G. Rowntree, 'Birth control in Britain', *Population Studies*, 15 (July and November 1961), 3–31, 121–60.

6. R. R. Sears, E. Maccoby and H. Levin, *Patterns of Child Rearing*, Row, Peterson, 1957.

7. M. L. Kohn and E. E. Carroll, 'Social class and the allocation of parental responsibilities', *Sociometry*, 23 (1960), 372–92.

CHAPTER 7

The Young

1. M. Abrams, *The Teenage Consumer*, London Press Exchange, Paper No. 5, July 1959, and *Teenage Consumer Spending in 1959: Middle Class and Working Class Boys and Girls*, London Press Exchange, January 1961.

2. M. Schofield, *The Sexual Behaviour of Young People*, Longmans, 1965.

3. M. P. Carter, *Home, School and Work*, Pergamon, 1962, particularly Ch. 6; and F. Musgrove, *Youth and the Social Order*, Routledge, 1964. See also E. M. Eppel and M. Eppel, *Adolescents and Morality*, Routledge, 1966.

4. R. K. Merton, 'Social Structure and Anomie' in *Social Theory & Social Structure*, Free Press, 1957

5. See particularly R. A. Cloward and L. Ohlin, *Delinquency and Opportunity*, Routledge, 1960; M. Clinard, ed., *Anomie and Social Deviation*, Free Press, 1964.

6. J. A. H. Lee, 'Motor-cycle accidents to male teenagers', *Proc. Roy. Soc. Med.* 56 (1963), 365–7.

7. P. Willmott, *Adolescent Boys of East London*, Routledge, 1966.

8. Central Advisory Council for Education—England, *15 to 18*, vol. II, pp. 81 ff., H.M.S.O. 1960.

The Old

9. P. Townsend, *The Family Life of Old People*, Routledge, 1957 (also in Penguin); in particular, but also the other Institute studies listed in the Introduction.

10. P. Townsend, *The Last Refuge*, Routledge, 1962.

11. P. Townsend and D. Wedderburn, *The Aged in the Welfare State*, Occasional Papers in Social Administration No. 14, 1965. Ministry of Pensions & National Insurance, *Financial and other circumstances of Retirement Pensioners*, H.M.S.O. 1966.

12. *Report of the Departmental Committee into the Impact of Rates in Households*, Cmnd. 2582, H.M.S.O. 1965.

13. F. Le Gros Clark, *Ageing in Industry*, Nuffield, 1955, and *Growing Old in a Mechanized World*, Nuffield, 1960. See also *Reasons Given for Retiring or Continuing at Work*, Ministry of Pensions and National Insurance, H.M.S.O., 1954; B. Shenfield, *Social Policies for Old Age*, Routledge, 1957. Unfortunately there is no up-to-date book on this.

CHAPTER 8

1. Ministry of Labour, *Statistics on Incomes, Prices, Employment and Production*, Table D.1.

2. S. de Grazia, *Of Time Work and Leisure*, Twentieth Century Fund, 1962. See also N. Anderson, *Work and Leisure*, Routledge, 1961.

3. H. T. Himmelweit, A. N. Oppenheim and P. Vince, *Television and the Child*, O.U.P. 1958.

4. H. J. Gans, 'Popular cultures in America: social problems in a mass society or social asset in a pluralist society?' in H. Becker, ed., *Social Problems: A Modern Approach*, Wiley, 1966.

5. P. Whannel and S. Hall, *The Popular Arts*, Pantheon, 1964.

6. R. Williams, *The Long Revolution*, Pelican, 1961.

7. T. Bottomore, 'Social stratification in voluntary organisations', in D. V. Glass, ed., *Social Mobility in Britain*, Routledge, 1954.

CHAPTER 9

Religion
1. G. Gorer, *Exploring English Character*, Cresset, 1955 (see Introduction).

2. B. Wilson, *Religion in Secular Society*, New Thinkers Library No. 15, Watts, 1966.

Politics

3. H. Durant, 'Voting behaviour in Britain', in R. Rose, ed., *Studies in British Politics*, Macmillan, 1966. Other references to poll figures are also taken from this article, or from Mark Abrams, 'Social trends and electoral behaviour' in the same symposium.

4. R. Rose, *Politics in England*, Faber, 1965.

5. W. Runciman, *Relative Deprivation and Social Justice*, Routledge, 1966.

6. R. R. Alford, *Party and Society*, Murray, 1964.

CHAPTER 10

1. H. Wilson, *Delinquency and Parental Neglect*, Allen & Unwin, 1962; A. F. Philp, *Family Failure*, Faber, 1963.

Crime

2. M. Gold, 'Undetected delinquent behaviour', *J. Res. Crim. Delinq.* 3 (Jan. 1966), 27–46.

3. See N. Walker, *Crime and Punishment in Britain*, Edinburgh University Press, 1965, a general book on the subject; and Home Office, *The Sentence of the Court*, H.M.S.O. 1964, the last part of which reports a large scale comparative study of sentencing.

4. T. C. Willett, *Criminal on the Road*, Tavistock, 1964.

Drugs : alcohol : road accidents

5. *Reports of the Committee on Dangerous Drugs* (Braine Committee), H.M.S.O. 1960, 1961, 1965. See also P. Laurie, *Drugs*, Penguin, 1967.

6. L. G. Norman, *Road Traffic Accidents*, World Health Organisation, Public Health Papers No. 12, 1962.

7. G. Prys Williams, *Decade of Drunkenness*, Christian Economic and Social Research Foundation, 1965. This is a temperance body, but the pamphlet has a useful collation of the statistics; F. H. Mclintock, *Crimes of Violence*, Macmillan, 1963.

Illegitimacy

8. V. Wimperis, *The Unmarried Mother and Her Child*, Allen & Unwin, 1960.

9. J. Spence *et al.*, *A Thousand Families in Newcastle-on-Tyne*, O.U.P. 1954; F. W. J. Miller *et al.*, *Growing Up in Newcastle-on-Tyne*, O.U.P. 1960.

Marriage breakdown

10. J. H. Wallis and H. S. Booker, *Marriage Counselling*, Routledge, 1958.

11. G. Rowntree and N. H. Carrier, 'The resort to divorce in England and Wales 1858–1957', *Population Studies* 11 (1958), 188–233; G. Rowntree, 'Some aspects of marriage breakdown in Britain during the last thirty years', *Population Studies* 18 (1964), 147–63. See also O. R. MacGregor, *Divorce in England*, Heinemann, 1957.

12. Registrar General's *Statistical Review of England and Wales*, Pt III, *Commentary*, H.M.S.O. 1963, Tables C21, C30.

13. M. Wynn, *Fatherless Families*, M. Joseph, 1962.

14. P. Marris, *Widows and Their Families*, Routledge, 1958; *Report by the Government Actuary on the Third Quinquennial Review*, *National Insurance Acts, 1946–1964*, H.M.S.O. 1964.

15. P. G. Gray and E. A. Parr, *Children in Care and the Recruitment of Foster Parents*, Government Social Survey, 1957.

16. Annual Returns of Children in the Care of Local Authorities, H.M.S.O.

17. M. Wynn, *op. cit.*

CHAPTER II

1. 'Forecasts of the working population 1966–81', *Ministry of Labour Gazette*, Nov. 1966, pp. 718–21; W. Beckerman *et al.*, *The British Economy in 1975*, C.U.P. 1965.

2. Useful discussions of reference groups are to be found in R. K. Merton, *Social Theory and Social Structure*, Free Press, 1957, Chs VIII and IX, and in W. G. Runciman, *Relative Deprivation and Social Justice*, Routledge, 1966.

3. J. H. Goldthorpe and D. Lockwood, 'Affluence and the British class structure', *Soc. Rev.* 11 (1963), 133–63.

4. J. Goldthorpe, D. Lockwood, F. Bechhofer and D. Platt, 'The

affluent worker and the thesis of embourgeoisement: some preliminary research findings', *Sociology* 1 (1967), 11–31.

5. H. L. Wilensky, 'Work as a social problem', in H. S. Becker, ed., *Social Problems: A modern Approach*, Wiley, 1966.

6. J. N. Morgan *et al.*, *Income and Welfare in the United States*, McGraw-Hill, 1962. Ch. 16. Table 16–18.

7. B. Bernstein, 'Social class and linguistic development', in A. H. Halsey *et al.*, ed., *Education, Economy and Society*, Free Press, 1961. Since 1961, the terminology has changed to 'restricted' and 'elaborated codes'.

8. R. Titmuss, *Essays on the Welfare State*, Unwin, 1958. pp. 32–3

Index